5.00

D1485630

A TASTE OF THE TROPICS

A TASTE OF THE TROPICS

SUSAN PARKINSON and **PEGGY STACY**

MILLS & BOON LIMITED, LONDON

First published 1972 by Mills & Boon Limited,
17–19 Foley Street, London W1A, 1DR.

© *1972 Susan Parkinson and Peggy Stacy*

All rights reserved. No portion of this book may be repro-
duced in any form (except by a reviewer who may wish to
quote brief passages in connection with a review) or stored
in a retrieval system, or transmitted in any form or by any
means, electronic, mechanical, photocopying, recording
or otherwise, without the prior permission of the publisher.

ISBN 0 263 05152 8

PRINTED IN GREAT BRITAIN
BY EBENEZER BAYLIS AND SON LTD.
THE TRINITY PRESS, WORCESTER, AND LONDON

Contents

5

Note: more detailed lists are given at the beginning of each section.

Acknowledgements

We would like to thank the following people who have provided useful ideas and recipes which have been included in this book.

Mrs Gill Baker for imaginative methods of using tropical foods in western recipes. Colonel Ottaway for his recipe Chicken Suvu. Miss Savita Tikaram and Mrs Margaret Wilson for suggestions concerning Indian dishes. Dr Lindsay Verrier for the coconut fish pâté recipe and many other friends who have provided ideas and suggestions.

Mr Robert Stone for the drawings of fish and Mr Maxwell Robinson, Dr Pagden and the Fiji School of Medicine for the photographs. We are greatly indebted to the late Adi Laisa Ganilau MBE for her advice concerning the methods of preparing many traditional Fijian fish, vegetable and coconut dishes which are in this book.

We give grateful thanks to Mrs Margaret Dawes and Mrs Maureen Taylor for typing the manuscript.

Foreword

In bygone days the thought of tropical foods brought to mind a picture of ships laden with oranges, sugar and spices, sailing for the first time into the harbours of the Old World. These ships of history came from the exotic tropical Islands of the West Indies and Indonesia where tea, coffee and spices were found in abundance. The tales of these early trading expeditions leave us with a picture of such countries yielding a veritable cornucopia of exotic foods. We imagine ourselves on white palm-fringed beaches, plucking ripe bananas from the trees, whilst coconuts fall at our feet.

While some of these catering dreams may be hard to realise in tropical countries today, a knowledge of the foods which grow in hot climates can yield exciting results to the inhabitants, the new-comer, the tourist and the housewife living in a temperate country.

In the markets we find a strange variety of foods that were never mentioned in the travellers' tales. There is a profusion of pumpkins together with some varieties of temperate-climate vegetables which modern science has adapted to grow in hot climates. Some of these are quite new to the people of the country, who may have to learn their uses.

The stranger arriving on tropical shores may have her curiosity aroused by the sight of okra, capsicums and guavas which lie in colourful heaps amongst root vegetables of unusual shapes and bunches of exotic green leaves. Equally bewildered may be the housewife in a temperate country who finds many of these foods now made available to her local greengrocer by air transport from the tropics.

Apart from the need to learn about the uses of these new foods, the bewildered housewife soon realises that food preparation in hot climates is fraught with problems. Some temperate-climate recipes do not respond as well as others in the high heat and humidity, but in most cases a good product can be achieved if the appropriate recipe and method are selected. For example good pastry can be made in the heat of a tropical summer if a particular skill is applied.

Hot weather cooking can be interesting and rewarding, but the most enthusiastic gourmet will rebel at the thought of long hours in the kitchen. The aim of this book is to introduce recipes which give good results, without involving a great deal of time and effort. All the dishes are suitable for tropical menus and can be made from available foods at a reasonable cost.

In a few recipes the preparation may at first glance appear involved, as in the delicious Chicken Suvu or Eggplant hors d'oeuvre, but on closer examination it will be seen that with a little planning, these dishes may be achieved with ease. The preparation is done in stages, with little last minute cooking.

The ideas for this recipe book have been gathered and developed from many hot countries. Many originate in the Pacific Islands, and some have been newly created for inclusion in the following pages.

Introductory Information

Authors' Note

The recipes have been set out with the ingredients listed at the side. At a quick glance you can determine if all components are available. The quantities have been written into the body of the recipe in order to avoid confusion when the same ingredient is used more than once.

On page 12 you will find a list of references which will aid in making substitutions and help to clarify unfamiliar items. Special note should be taken of fruit, vegetable and fish charts available on pages 75, 118 and 158, which will aid familiarisation. These charts will be of particular advantage to those living in more temperate climates where some of the listed ingredients may not be as easily found.

Page 12 shows the exact quantities we have assumed for standard measurement as regrettably they often vary from place to place. Abbreviations used throughout the book are also stated.

A handy list of equivalents is given on page 13 and common household substitutes on page 12.

Weights, measures, substitutes, equivalents, temperatures

All measurements are level

     1t (teaspoon)   = 5 millilitres
     1T (Tablespoon) = 15   „
     3t (teaspoon)   = 1 T (Tablespoon)
    16 T = 1 c (cup)
     1 c = 8 oz (ounces) liquid measure = 225 millilitres
     1 pt (pint) = 20 oz liquid measure   = 570   „
     1 oz   = 25 g
     1 pound (16 oz)   = 455 g

All-purpose (plain) flour is used in recipes unless otherwise stated. Margarine may be substituted for butter if desired. Margarine is preferred to butter in pastry.
Oil, dripping or lard may be used for deep fat frying.

SUBSTITUTES

4 oz sour cream	4 oz tinned cream or very thick fresh cream plus 1 t lime or lemon juice.
1 c beef or chicken stock	1 c water plus 1 chicken or beef cube.
Soy sauce	If using a thick strong sauce; halve given quantity in recipe. Japanese soy sauce is much lighter in colour and has less flavour than Chinese soy sauce.
Chilli sauce	Tabasco or Chinese chilli sauce or fresh, red chillies ground and mixed with a little salad oil may be used.
Hoisin sauce	Available in Chinese grocery shops. There is no substitute. If not available omit from recipe and increase other flavours.
Parmesan cheese	Romano or dried Cheddar cheese may be substituted.
Dalo (taro) breadfruit, cassava, vudi (cooking banana)	Potato may be substituted quite successfully.

12

Chopped or puréed Dalo (taro leaves) or bhagi	Spinach.
Whole rou rou (taro) leaves	Large Chinese cabbage or English cabbage leaves.
Milk and products	1 cup whole milk = 3 tablespoons skimmed milk powder, 2 tablespoons butter and 1 cup water or 4 level packed tablespoons whole milk powder plus 1 cup water.
	1 cup sour milk = 1 tablespoon vinegar or lemon juice plus milk to equal 1 cup.
	$\frac{1}{2}$ cup sour cream = 1 teaspoon lemon juice to 4 oz (100 g) tinned or thick fresh cream.
	Evaporated milk is comparable to unsweetened condensed milk.
	"Rich milk" is comparable to evaporated milk or $\frac{1}{2}$ milk, $\frac{1}{2}$ cream.
Flour	1 cup cake flour = 1 cup plain or all-purpose flour minus 2 tablespoons plus 2 tablespoons cornflour.
	1 cup self raising flour = 1 cup all-purpose flour plus $1\frac{1}{2}$ teaspoons baking powder.
	2 tablespoons flour = 1 tablespoon cornflour for thickening.
Yeast	1 ounce fresh yeast = 1 tablespoon dry yeast.
	1 package yeast = 1 tablespoon.
Chocolate	1 ounce chocolate = 3 tablespoons cocoa plus 2 teaspoons fat.

EQUIVALENTS

Butter	1 pound = 2 cups.
	1 ounce = 2 tablespoons
Margarine	1 8-ounce package = 1 cup.
	For ease in measuring the package may be divided in halves or thirds depending on what is required. This is a particularly easy way of measuring the margarine for scones or pastry.

13

Sugar	1 pound of soft brown sugar = $2\frac{1}{4}$ cups firmly packed.
	1 pound granulated or caster sugar = 2 cups
	1 pound icing sugar = $3\frac{1}{2}$ cups.
Egg	1 medium = $\frac{1}{4}$ cup.
	3 yolks = $\frac{1}{4}$ cup.
	2 whites = $\frac{1}{4}$ cup.
Flour	1 pound = 4 cups sifted once before measuring.
	4 ounces = 1 cup.
	1 ounce = 4 tablespoons or $\frac{1}{4}$ cup.
Rice	1 pound uncooked = 2 cups.
Bread crumbs	1 pound = 4 cups of fine crumbs.
Bulk cheese	1 pound = 4 cups coarsely grated.
Mixed fruit	1 pound = $2\frac{1}{2}$ cups.

OVEN TEMPERATURES

These have been given in Degrees F throughout. Practical equivalents are as follows:

Degrees F	Degrees C	Gas Mark	Description
150	70		
175	80		
200	100	$\frac{1}{4}$	
225	110	$\frac{1}{2}$	very slow
250	130	$\frac{3}{4}$	
275	140	1	slow
300	150	2	moderately slow
325	170	3	
350	180	4	moderate
375	190	5	moderately hot
400	200	6	
425	220	7	hot
450	230	8	very hot
475	240	9	

Seasoning

The art of good cooking lies in an ability to develop subtle flavours in food. This is usually achieved by the careful use of herbs and spices.

Seasonings should be used to develop the flavour of the main food in a recipe—not to mask it.

Great care must always be taken in seasoning. Overflavoured food is spoilt food. It is wise to underseason until one is confident in the use of herbs and spices.

Ground spices and herbs give up their aroma more quickly than their whole counterparts. For this reason these should be added near the end of the cooking time in a long cooking dish, otherwise add with the salt. Whole spices are added at the beginning of cooking, and for convenience, often tied up in a piece of cheesecloth.

When using unfamiliar spices and herbs $\frac{1}{4}$ teaspoon per pound of meat is an average amount to experiment with; remember that 1 tablespoon of chopped fresh herbs is equal to $\frac{1}{2}$ teaspoon of dried or $\frac{1}{4}$ teaspoon of ground herbs.

To assist you in your choice of possible spices and herbs for a particular dish we have included the following chart.

BEEF

Pot roast	allspice, ginger, marjoram.
Stews and casseroles	basil, bay leaf, celery seed/salt, chilli powder, cinnamon, clove, cumin, mace, mustard, nutmeg, oregano, parsley, poppy seed, savory, thyme.
Steak	garlic, monosodium glutamate.
Oxtail	bay leaf, celery salt, garlic.
Heart	bay leaf
Liver	caraway, cardamom, cinnamon.
Corned-beef	bay leaf, clove, peppercorn.
Kidney	bay leaf, caraway.
General	black pepper, cayenne pepper, coriander, dill seed, mace, mustard, sage, tamarind, soy sauce.

15

VEAL

Casseroles and stews	thyme.
Breaded	marjoram.
Stuffing	parsley, sage, savory, thyme.
General	paprika, parsley, tarragon.

LAMB

Lamb chops	basil, cinnamon, dill.
Stuffing	savory.
Roast	celery seed/salt, garlic, rosemary.
Lamb stews and casseroles	bay leaf, garlic, thyme.
Mutton	caraway, marjoram, thyme.
General	marjoram, mint, paprika, parsley.

PORK

Roast	caraway, clove, coriander, fennel.
Chops	cinnamon, paprika.
Ham	clove, mustard.
General	allspice, cardamom, celery seed/salt, cinnamon, cumin, ginger, sage, savory, soy sauce, apple, orange, pineapple, other acid fruits, onion, vinegar.

FISH

Baked	clove, coriander, marjoram, sage, savory, thyme.
Grilled or fried	marjoram, rosemary, savory, thyme.
Boiled or steamed	clove, dill, fennel, marjoram, tarragon, thyme.
Sauce	marjoram, mint.
General	allspice, bay leaf, cayenne pepper, celery salt/seed, mace, parsley, turmeric, white pepper.

SHELLFISH

Crayfish	tarragon.
Crab	mustard seed, garlic.
General	cumin, oregano, paprika, sweet basil.

CHICKEN

Stuffing	coriander, marjoram, oregano, poppy seed, sage, savory, thyme.
Stewed or fricasséed	bay leaf, celery seed/salt, mace, marjoram, thyme.
Roasting or grilling	garlic, marjoram, savory.
General	basil, garlic, ginger, mace, monosodium glutamate, nutmeg, paprika, parsley, pepper, rosemary, saffron, sesame seed, tarragon.

VEGETABLES

Beans	basil, chilli powder, cinnamon, clove, cumin, curry powder, dill, garlic, mint, mustard, nutmeg, oregano, paprika, parsley, savory, sesame seed, thyme.
Chocho	cinnamon, dill, garlic, mace, marjoram, mustard, nutmeg, paprika, parsley, savory, tarragon, thyme.
Duruka	caraway seed, celery seed/salt, chilli powder, dill, mint, mustard, paprika, savory.
Eggplant	allspice, anise, bay leaf, chilli powder, coriander, garlic, parsley, sage.
Creeping spinach Indian spinach Bele Chinese cabbage Taro leaves	basil, dill, nutmeg, tarragon.
Taro leaves Sweet potato or pumpkin tops	basil, oregano, rosemary, tarragon.
Water cress Ota	basil, dill, parsley, tarragon.
Gourds	basil, garlic, marjoram, mustard, savory, thyme.
Kohlrabi	chilli powder, dill, mace, mustard, nutmeg, tarragon.
Okra	bay leaf, basil, celery seed/salt, chilli powder, curry powder, garlic, mustard, parsley, thyme.

Paw paw, green	allspice, basil, cinnamon, clove, ginger, mustard, nutmeg, savory, sesame seed.
Breadfruit Cooking banana Cassava Dalo ni Tana Dalo (taro) Yams	bay leaf, caraway, celery seed/salt, coriander, dill, fennel seed, garlic, mace, marjoram, mustard, paprika, parsley, poppy seed.
Kumala Kawai	allspice, cinnamon, clove, ginger, mace, nutmeg, poppy seed.
White radish	caraway, mint, mustard, oregano, parsley, poppy seed, rosemary, sage.

Indian Curry powders and Masalas

A masala is a basic mixture of spices which varies greatly according to individual tastes and to the different regions of India. When turmeric is added, it then becomes known as a curry powder.

A simple masala would be coriander and peppercorn, ground and blended, using approximately 3 times as much coriander as black pepper. Other simple masalas may be coriander, fenugreek and mustard seed or coriander, peppercorn, cinnamon, cumin and fennel; for example—3 T coriander seeds, 1 T cumin, 1 T black pepper, 1 t mustard seed, 1 t cloves, 1 T ground ginger—or use crushed fresh ginger, 1 T ground turmeric.

For this masala grind the whole dry spices, and add the turmeric at the end.

Garam Masala, a fragrant strong mixture which is suitable for meat, fried and braised foods is as follows:

6 T	black peppercorns
5 T	caraway seed
$1\frac{3}{4}$ T	cinnamon stick (finely broken)
6 T	coriander
$1\frac{3}{4}$ T	cloves
$1\frac{1}{2}$ T	cardamom seeds.
	prepare as directed under preparation of masala (below), grind and blend.

With the basic masala of coriander and peppercorn some of the

18

following spices are most commonly added, producing the different curries.

Beef	bay leaf or curry leaf (tejpati), cardamom, chilli, cinnamon, clove, cumin, garlic, ginger, turmeric.
Chicken	cardamom, chilli, clove, cumin, fennel, garlic, ginger, turmeric.
Mutton, lamb	bay leaf, chilli, cumin, garlic, ginger, turmeric.
Fish	anise, cardamom seed, cinnamon, clove, fennel, ginger, saffron, turmeric.
Vegetable	chilli, cumin, garlic, ginger, mint, turmeric.
Egg	chilli, turmeric.

PREPARATION OF MASALA AND SPICES IN READINESS FOR CURRY PREPARATION

Wash spices, dry in the sun and then in the oven at 200° F until thoroughly heated and dried to a crisp. Grind, using a spice or coffee grinder, or pound in a mortar.

The basic masala of coriander and black pepper may be mixed and kept in an airtight jar. It is suggested that cinnamon, cumin, fennel, mustard seed and fenugreek be ground and kept separate, along with a supply of turmeric, fresh garlic, ginger and chilli which may be crushed as required. Cardamom seed, bay leaf, anise seed may be used whole. The variation in your curries may then be endless. Remember that good airtight glass jars are necessary for storing spices and herbs; once ground the aromatic flavour is soon lost when exposed to the air.

In tropical countries many of the spice shops are run by Indian people. For this reason the Hindustani names of some of the spices may be helpful.

Curry leaves	Tejpati
Anise seed	Saunf
Black pepper	Kala mirchi
Cardamom	Elachi
Chillies	Mirchi
Cinnamon	Dhal cheene
Cloves	Laong
Coriander	Dhuniah
Cumin	Jeera

Ginger, green	Udruk
Fenugreek	Methee
Garlic	Lusson
Mace	Jaffatry
Mint	Pootheena
Mustard	Rai
Nutmeg	Jaiphul
Poppy seed	Kus kus
Saffron	Zuffron
Turmeric	Huldee

THE USE OF SPICES

Whole spices like cloves and cinnamon stick are often bruised with a heavy spoon to release the flavour. In curries, pilaus and similar dishes, spices are sautéd in oil or ghee at a low to medium temperature to develop the flavours. Care must be taken not to overheat the oil or ghee as this will spoil the flavour.

Large pieces of whole spice may be removed before serving to improve appearance. Smaller spices like cardamom seeds or cumin may be left in dishes.

How to Prepare Coconut Cream

Select mature, but not old, coconuts. Look to see that the "eyes" are not sprouting, and shake to find out whether there is water inside the nut. An old dry nut is not fit to use. Crack the nut in half by giving a sharp tap with a heavy knife in the middle. Pull the two halves apart.

The coconut water from a mature nut has a sweet flavour. It may be chilled and used for drinking or used in the preparation of the cream. The water from green nuts is preferred for drinks.

Take the two coconut halves and grate out the flesh with a coconut grater. Alternatively cut the flesh out of the shell and grate on a coarse household grater.

The richness of the coconut cream is determined by the amount of water added to the grated flesh. For a thick rich cream add 1 T water to 1 c grated coconut, for a medium rich cream add $\frac{1}{2}$ c water to 1 c grated coconut.

Squeeze the grated coconut with the water, and then place in a square of muslin or nylon net. Squeeze out the cream using a wringing action.

Another method is to place the grated coconut and water in a blender, reduce to a pulp and then pour the pulp into a fine strainer and press out the cream.

Coconut cream contains some protein. When boiled the protein curdles and separates out. This does not matter in some dishes, e.g. rou rou p. 53 but in others such as fish soup p. 42 the consistency and flavour are spoiled by boiling the cream. The addition of a little cornflour helps to prevent curdling. It is best to cook the majority of coconut cream dishes at simmering point.

A Substitute for fresh coconuts

Use $1\frac{1}{2}$ c desiccated coconut mixed with $\frac{1}{2}$ c warm milk. Leave for half an hour and then squeeze out the cream.

Party Food

22

Party food is interesting to prepare. It is colourful and provides variety from our daily fare. Delicious savouries and sandwiches can be easily prepared at reasonable cost. One does not need to be an expert cook to achieve good results.

In this modern world of prepackaged meals, the interest which a hostess shows in her guests by preparing her own party food is always appreciated.

A golden rule for hostesses living in hot climates is to plan the party menu well in advance. Pastry or choux paste cases and toasted or fried bread canapés may all be made several days ahead and stored in airtight tins. Savoury butters keep well in the refrigerator or freezer. A basic white sauce, made the day before and chilled, may be mixed with a variety of different flavourings, and spooned into prepared cases on the day of the party.

Savouries requiring last minute baking or grilling, may be made a day or even weeks before they are required, and deep frozen. These may then be popped in the oven or under the griller just before serving. Such procedures are well worth considering as this method of approach ensures that the hostess appears at her party cool and calm.

How much food should be prepared for a drinks party?

The number of dishes will depend on the time of the day and the number of guests. For drinks before seven, we suggest a total of 6 to 7 savouries or sandwiches per guest. This does not include nuts or chips. For the pre-lunch party, savouries may be reduced to 2 or 3 and about 2 larger sandwiches.

Successful party food must be colourful and well flavoured. It is wise to keep the variety of the items down to a number which can be easily managed. A few kinds of really delicious savouries or sandwiches are infinitely preferable to a greater variety prepared in haphazard fashion.

In this chapter we present a number of food ideas which may be produced with reasonable effort and cost in most parts of the world.

Chips

Delicious crisp chips can be made from many starchy roots and fruits which are available in the Tropics.

The chips should be fried in a very hot flavourless salad oil, in a heavy deep saucepan. After cooking, chips should be lifted out and put in a strainer to remove surplus oil and then placed on absorbent paper. Alternatively use a frying basket.

The thick type of chips should be kept hot and served as soon as possible. Thin chips may be cooled and stored in a sealed container for future use.

Thick chips

Thick chips may be made from cooked taro, breadfruit, cassava or kumala (sweet potato). Bake, boil or steam any of the preceding vegetables till soft, but still firm. Cut into

24

pieces about $1-1\frac{1}{2}$ inches long and $\frac{1}{4}$ inch thick. Fry in hot oil till crisp and brown. Dust with salt and pepper.

Note: If the above vegetables are not available, use potato and do not precook before frying.

Thin chips

Thin chips may be made from kumalas, green bananas and cooking bananas (vudi). Green bananas may be peeled like a potato using a paring knife. Rub a little oil on the hands to prevent staining.

Cut very thin slices with a potato peeler or a very sharp knife. Put slices to soak in a bowl of water for $\frac{1}{2}$ hour to draw out excess starch. Take out and dry on a cloth. Fry in hot oil until crisp and brown. Dust with salt and pepper just before serving. Do not add salt ahead of time as chips are inclined to go soft.

Cassava drops

Grate raw cassava on a fine grater and season with salt and pepper. Form into small round balls by gently rolling in the hands. Drop into hot oil and fry until golden brown.

Just before serving they may be sprinkled with additional salt or a little curry powder, ground cumin, basil or any other desired spices or herbs.

Hors d'oeuvres
FILLINGS FOR VOL-AU-VENT CASES

Patty or vol-au-vent cases may be filled with any of the following mixtures based on a plain white sauce. Allow 1 t of mixture per case. These fillings are also useful for pancakes—see Section 7.

Basic white sauce

butter
flour
salt and pepper
dry mustard
milk
Yield: $1\frac{1}{3}$ cups

Melt 3 T of butter in a saucepan. Stir in 3 T of flour with $\frac{1}{2}$ t salt, dash of pepper and $\frac{1}{2}$ t dry mustard.
Slowly stir in 1 c milk and cook over low heat until thick and smooth.
Allow to simmer 3 minutes.

Chilli crab

basic white sauce
crab
garlic
butter
chilli sauce
lemon juice
parsley
salt
Yield: 3 cups

Prepare Basic White Sauce.
Cook and prepare sufficient crab to yield $1\frac{1}{2}$ c. (Tinned crab may be substituted.) Chop 1 large clove of garlic finely. Fry in 1 T butter. Stir in crab and cook for 3 minutes. Add 2 t chilli sauce, 2 t lemon juice and 2 T finely chopped parsley. Cook for 1 minute more. Stir in sauce and check seasoning for salt.

Fish and stuffed olives

basic white sauce
white fish
garlic
butter
olives, stuffed
lemon juice
salt
pepper
Yield: 3 cups

Prepare Basic White Sauce.
Cook and prepare sufficient white fish to yield $1\frac{1}{2}$ c.
Finely chop 1 large clove of garlic. Fry in 1 T butter for 2–3 minutes. Stir in 6 finely chopped stuffed olives, 2 t lemon juice and the prepared fish. Cook over low heat for 2 minutes.
Stir in prepared sauce and re-season with salt and pepper if necessary.

Sockeye salmon and spring onion

basic white sauce
sockeye salmon
spring onion
lemon juice
salt
pepper
Yield: 2 cups

Prepare Basic White Sauce.
Drain and flake the sockeye salmon from 1 $7\frac{1}{2}$ oz tin. (220 g.)
Finely chop spring onions to yield 2 T. Stir salmon, spring onions and 2 t lemon juice into white sauce.
Season with salt and pepper.

Seafood dill

basic white sauce	Prepare Basic White Sauce.
prawns or white fish	Chop ½ c of cooked shelled prawns or
dill	cooked white fish.
lemon juice	Season white sauce with 1 t of chopped fresh
pepper	dill or ½ t of dried dill and 2 t of lemon juice.
chilli sauce	Further season with a little freshly ground
(optional)	pepper and chilli or tabasco sauce if
celery or cucumber	desired.
salt	Stir in prawns or white fish.
Yield: 2 cups	Just before serving add 1 T of finely
	chopped celery or cucumber and season to
	taste with salt.

Curried egg

basic white sauce	Prepare Basic White Sauce.
egg	Hard boil 2 eggs and chop finely.
curry powder	Add 1 t of curry powder, 1 t of finely
fresh coriander	chopped fresh coriander leaves and the
leaves	juice from 1 clove of garlic to white sauce.
garlic	Beat well. Add chopped egg and season
salt	with extra salt and pepper if required.
pepper	*Note :* If coriander leaves are not available,
Yield: 2 cups	1 T of finely chopped spring onions may
	be substituted.

Mushroom and kidney

basic white sauce	Prepare Basic White Sauce.
mushrooms	Chop and fry enough mushrooms to yield ½c.
bacon	Finely chop 1 rasher of bacon and sauté
kidney	until golden.
dry mustard	Clean and chop finely 1 lamb's kidney. Add
sherry (optional)	to bacon and sauté until tender. Season with
salt	½ t of mustard and 2 t of dry sherry. Stir in
Yield: 1½ cups	mushrooms.
	Combine mixture with ½ c of white sauce.
	Season to taste with salt.

Cheese and olives

basic white sauce	Prepare Basic White Sauce.
Cheddar cheese	To 1 c of white sauce, add ½ c of finely
stuffed olives	grated Cheddar cheese, ½ c of coarsely
cayenne pepper	chopped stuffed green olives and a dash of
salt	cayenne pepper. Season to taste with salt.
seafood	Fold in ½ c of flaked white fish, prawns or
Yield: 2¼ cups	crab.

Tomato and cheese

basic white sauce	Prepare Basic White Sauce.
Cheddar cheese	Grate ½ c Cheddar cheese. Flake sufficient
fish (white)	white fish to yield ½ cup.
tomato paste or	Beat 2 t tomato paste or 1 T tomato purée
tomato purée	into 1 c white sauce. Add 2 t sherry and the
sherry	juice from 1 small clove of garlic.
garlic	Mix in cheese and beat well. Fold in flaked
salt	fish. Season to taste with salt.
Yield: 2¼ cups	*Note:* Prawns may be substituted for fish.

Pacific Island filling

coconut cream	Prepare 1 c coconut cream.
cornflour	Mix 2 t cornflour with a little of the cream.
lemon juice	Stir into remaining cream in saucepan.
salt	Bring to boiling point, stirring constantly.
chilli or	Do not allow to actually boil. Add 2 to 3 t
tabasco sauce	lemon juice, ½ t salt, a little chilli or tabasco
(optional)	sauce and 1 t freshly chopped dill.
dill	½ c cooked prawns and ¼ c raw cucumber
seafood (optional)	cubes, or fish kokoda (p. 36), may be added
Yield: 2 cups	to the sauce.

Savoury chicken pieces

chicken	Cut 1 chicken into bite size pieces.
oil	Prepare a marinade from ¼ c of oil, 2 T
lemon juice	lemon juice, 2 t chopped fresh herbs, ½ t
fresh herbs	salt and a dash of pepper.
salt and pepper	Marinate chicken for 1 to 2 hours, remove
egg	and drain. Dip pieces of chicken in 1 beaten
water	egg to which 1 T of water has been added.
bread crumbs	Roll in 1 c dried bread crumbs mixed with

sesame seeds
oil
Serves: 10

2 T of sesame seeds. Chill for 1 hour. Fry in hot oil until golden brown. Transfer to wire rack and bake in 250–300° F oven for 20 minutes.
Serve hot on toothpicks.

Pineapple and bacon
pineapple
bacon
Yield: as desired

Cut fresh pineapple into wedges, or use tinned pineapple cubes.
Wrap 2 inch strips of bacon around pineapple and fasten with toothpicks. Grill until bacon is crisp and golden, turning frequently. Drain and serve immediately.

Banana and bacon
bananas
bacon
Yield: as desired

Cut just ripe, but still firm, bananas into 1 inch pieces. Wrap with 2 inch pieces of bacon and fasten with toothpicks.
Grill, turning frequently, or bake until bacon is golden.
Drain and serve immediately.

Petite drumsticks
chicken wings
eggs
flour
salt
dry sherry
oil
freshly ground
   black pepper
Serves: 10
Yield: 40 Petite
   Drumsticks

Take 2 lb of chicken wings (about 10 wings) and separate into joints, retaining the upper and middle sections. Discard wing tips. Separate the 2 bones of middle sections by prying apart, allowing the meat to cling to each bone. Push the meat down to one end of each bone section and twist meat around to form little drumsticks. Each chicken wing will yield 4 petite drumsticks.
Prepare a batter with 2 well beaten eggs, 6 T flour, 1 t salt and 1 T dry sherry.
Dip the meat end of drum sticks in batter and fry until golden in very hot deep oil. Just before serving sprinkle with freshly ground black pepper.
Serve hot or cold.

29

Stuffed eggs

In order to insure easy peeling use 3 day old eggs or add salt to cooking water. Hard boil, cool and peel eggs. Cut in half, remove yolks and reserve the whites. Place yolks in a bowl and mash well. Prepare in one of the given ways. Fill egg whites using 2 spoons or a pastry (piping) bag. Chill well before serving.

Plain devilled eggs

mayonnaise
eggs
salt
cayenne pepper
Serves: 24

Add 5 to 6 T mayonnaise to 12 well mashed yolks. Season to taste with salt and $\frac{1}{8}$ to $\frac{1}{4}$ t cayenne pepper.

Curried eggs with spring onions

mayonnaise
eggs
salt
cayenne pepper
curry powder
spring onions
Serves: 24

Add 5 to 6 T mayonnaise to 12 well mashed yolks. Season to taste with salt, $\frac{1}{8}$ to $\frac{1}{4}$ t cayenne pepper and $\frac{1}{2}$ to 1 t curry powder. Blend in 2 T finely chopped spring onions.

Anchovy caper eggs

eggs
anchovy sauce
capers
lemon juice
mayonnaise
salt
Serves: 24

Season 12 well mashed yolks with 1 T anchovy sauce, 2 T finely chopped capers and 1 to 2 t lemon juice. Thin to desired consistency with 4 to 5 T mayonnaise. Check seasoning and add salt if necessary.

Fresh herb eggs

mayonnaise
eggs
salt
cayenne pepper
fresh herbs
Serves: 24

Add 5 to 6 T mayonnaise to 12 well mashed yolks. Season with 1 t salt, $\frac{1}{8}$ t cayenne pepper and 1 T freshly chopped herbs (sage, thyme or basil).

Spinach eggs

*puréed spinach
    or greens*
eggs
onion
mayonnaise
salt
*freshly ground
    black pepper*
Serves: 24

Add $\frac{1}{4}$ c finely puréed spinach or other greens to 12 well mashed egg yolks. Blend in 1 T finely grated onion. Thin with a little mayonnaise if required and season to taste with 1 t salt and freshly ground black pepper.

Tomato eggs

tomato paste
onion
eggs
mayonnaise
salt
pepper
Serves: 24

Add 2 T tomato paste and 1 T finely grated onion to 12 well mashed egg yolks. Blend well and thin to desirable consistency with 2 to 3 T mayonnaise. Season to taste with 1 t salt and $\frac{1}{8}$ t pepper.

Savoury Butters, Spreads and Dips

BUTTERS

A well-flavoured savoury butter has many uses. For sandwiches some attractive combinations are:

    herb butter with egg filling
    lemon butter with cold fish
    garlic butter with rare beef and mustard
    garlic butter with salami, liver sausage or pâté
    anchovy butter with tomato filling.

It is important to see that the flavour of the butter blends with the sandwich filling. Butter must be well creamed by thoroughly beating before additional flavours are added.

31

Herb

fresh mixed herbs
butter
Yield: 1¼ cups

Add ¼ c finely chopped fresh mixed herbs, such as parsley, chives and mint, and ½ to 1 t of the strong flavoured herbs, such as sage, thyme or basil to ½ lb (¼ kg) butter.

Garlic

garlic
salt
butter
Yield: 1 cup

Crush 1 clove of garlic to a paste with ½ t salt, add to ½ lb (¼ kg) butter.

Lemon

lemon
butter
Yield: 1 cup

Add 1 T lemon juice and ½ t grated lemon rind to ½ lb (¼ kg) butter.

Anchovy

anchovy sauce
lemon juice
butter
Yield: 1 cup

Add 2 T anchovy sauce and 1 T lemon juice to ½ lb (¼ kg) butter.

Mustard

French mustard
butter
Yield: 1 cup

Add 2 t of French prepared mustard to ½ lb (¼ kg) butter.

Savoury butters used as a topping for canapés

Butters may be thickly spread on biscuits or bread shapes and garnished with a suitably flavoured meat, fish or vegetable.

Savoury hot bread

Loaves of French bread may be cut diagonally to the base crust in thick slices. Spread each slice with butter, wrap in greaseproof paper and leave for several hours. (This improves the flavour.) Remove paper and bake at 350° F till crisp; about 20 minutes.

32

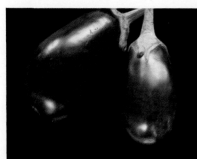

BAIGAN

CHINESE CABBAGE

SWEET PEPPER

CREEPING SPINACH

MANGOSTENE

ACEROLA

INDIAN CHERRY

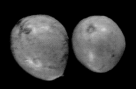

BRAZILIAN CHERRY

WI

SPREADS

Tuna cheese

tin tuna
grated cheese
stuffed olives
lemon juice
mayonnaise
salt
pepper
Yield: 1 cup

Flake a 7-oz (175 g) tin of drained tuna. Mix in ½ c finely grated cheese, ¼ c finely chopped stuffed olives, 1 t lemon juice, add ¼ c mayonnaise or sufficient to reach desired consistency. Season to taste with salt and freshly ground black pepper.

Blue cheese

blue cheese
cream cheese
top of the milk
spring onion
salt
pepper
Yield: ¾ cup

Crumble 1 oz (25 g) blue cheese. Cream 4 oz (100 g) cream cheese with 1 T top of the milk. Stir in crumbled blue cheese and 1 T finely chopped spring onions. Season to taste with salt and pepper.

Red bean

onion
garlic
oil
red kidney beans
tomato paste or
 purée
basil
salt
Yield: 1½ cups

Chop ½ onion finely and crush 1 small clove of garlic. Sauté in 1 T oil until soft. Stir in 1 c cooked kidney beans (canned beans are excellent). Add 1 T tomato paste or 2 T tomato purée and 1 t chopped fresh basil or ½ t dried basil. Simmer for 3 minutes. Purée in a blender or rub through a sieve. Add extra liquid from the beans to produce a creamy spread of the right consistency. Season to taste with salt.

Eggplant "caviar"

eggplant
olive oil
garlic
lemon juice
salt
black pepper
Yield: 1 cup

Bake 1 large eggplant in the oven at 300° F until soft. Scoop the flesh out of the skin. Heat 1 T olive (or salad) oil and sauté 1 small crushed clove of garlic in it. Combine eggplant with oil and garlic. Simmer a few minutes. Season with 1 to 2 t lemon juice, salt and freshly ground black pepper.

c

Ham and olive

ham
olives
dry mustard
milk
basic white sauce
Yield: 2 cups

Mince ¼ lb (100 g) lean ham and chop ¼ c olives finely. Mix 1 t dry mustard with 2 t milk. Combine all ingredients with 1 c Basic White Sauce. Mix well.

Pâté

lamb's liver
bacon
black pepper
butter
garlic
nutmeg
brandy
sugar
salt
Yield: 2 cups

Prepare 1 lb (½ kg) lamb's liver by removing the skin and any tough blood vessels. Put in a casserole, cover with 2 rashers of bacon and season with freshly ground black pepper. Cover and bake in a 250–300° F oven for ¾ hour. Cool and put through the mincer twice or reduce to a fine pulp in a blender.

Beat ½ lb (¼ kg) butter to a cream. Add ½ small crushed clove of garlic, ¼ t grated nutmeg, ½ t freshly ground black pepper, ½ c brandy, 1 t sugar and salt to taste.

Beat butter mixture thoroughly into liver and chill.

This pâté may be deep frozen and used as required. The flavour may be varied by using less brandy and a little more nutmeg and black pepper.

Smoked tuna pâté

smoked tuna
coconut cream
chilli
lemon juice
monosodium
   glutamate
gelatine
Yield: 1½ cups

Remove skin and bones from 8 oz (200 g) smoked tuna. Add 1 c coconut cream, 1 small chilli, 1 T lemon juice, ¼ t monosodium glutamate. Put all ingredients in a blender and leave till well mixed but not reduced to a purée. Dissolve 1 t gelatine in 2 t water. Mix well and chill.

Serve on biscuits or brown bread.

Variations: Use tabasco sauce in place of chilli; use any other good smoked fish in place of tuna.

34

DIPS

Guacamole

avocado
cream cheese
mayonnaise
chilli powder
onion
garlic
lemon juice
tomato
salt
Yield: 2 cups

Peel and mash 1 large avocado. Blend $\frac{1}{4}$ c cream cheese, $\frac{1}{3}$ c mayonnaise, $\frac{1}{2}$ t chilli powder, 2 t minced onion, 1 small crushed clove of garlic, 2 t lemon juice and 1 medium size tomato peeled and chopped. Add to avocado and season with salt. Mix well. Stand for an hour before serving to develop the flavour. Good with something salty like potato crisps.

Coconut, fish and garlic

sour cream
lime or lemon juice
coconut
fish, white
garlic
salt
pepper
Yield: $1\frac{1}{4}$ cups

To $\frac{1}{2}$ c sour cream add 1 t lime or lemon juice, $\frac{1}{4}$ c firmly packed freshly grated coconut, $\frac{1}{2}$ c finely flaked cooked white fish and 1 small crushed clove of garlic. Season to taste with salt and pepper. Mix well. Refrigerate for 2 hours before serving to allow the full flavour to develop.

Cheesey silverside

cream cheese
onion
lime or lemon juice
salt
monosodium
  glutamate
cayenne pepper
silverside
top milk
Yield: $1\frac{1}{4}$ cups

Cream $\frac{1}{2}$ c cream cheese. Season with 1 T minced onion, 1 t lime or lemon juice, $\frac{1}{4}$ t salt, $\frac{1}{4}$ t monosodium glutamate and $\frac{1}{8}$ t cayenne pepper. Stir in $\frac{1}{2}$ c finely minced cooked silverside and thin to desirable consistency with top milk ($\frac{1}{4}$ c or slightly more). Check and adjust seasoning if required. Refrigerate for at least 2 hours before serving to allow full flavour to develop.

Yoghurt and cucumber

cucumber
salt
yoghurt
garlic
dill or chives
chilli (optional)

Take $\frac{1}{2}$ a medium sized peeled cucumber and grate. Sprinkle with $\frac{1}{2}$ t salt and leave to drain in a strainer. Mix with 1 c thick yoghurt and $\frac{1}{2}$ clove garlic crushed in $\frac{1}{2}$ t salt and 1 t fresh dill or chives chopped. Chill well.

35

Kora (Fermented Coconut)

coconuts
seawater
salt
pepper or chillies
lemon juice
onion
Yield: 1 cup

Grate 1 coconut and squeeze out the cream. Mix the grated flesh with 1 c boiled seawater or 1 c water plus 1 T salt. Put in a jar, cover and leave in a warm place. Stir daily for 1 week.

At the end of the fermentation period, the coconut should have a soft smooth consistency. Strain off the liquid.

Squeeze the cream from 1 grated coconut (do not add water). Mix the cream with the fermented coconut flesh. Flavour with pepper or chopped chillies, 2 t lemon juice and 1 t grated onion.

Serve with fish, on biscuits as cheese-like spread or in Kora Banana Ota (p. 59).

Notes: If previously prepared Kora is available, 1 t may be stirred into the grated coconut before allowing it to ferment. This controls and speeds up fermentation (5 to 6 days). Kora should not be attempted unless fresh coconut is available.

Cocktails

Kokoda (Basic recipe)

A fish with fine but firm white flesh and not too many bones, is best. Walu, Saqa and Kanaci are some of the favourite fish in Fiji.

The coconut sauce should be delicately flavoured with onion, lemon, a little chilli and possibly ginger or dill.

white fish
lemon or lime juice
coconut
lemon
onion
chilli
salt
water
dill (optional)

Remove the bones and skin from $1\frac{1}{2}$ lb ($\frac{3}{4}$ kg) of fish and cut into $\frac{1}{4}$ inch cubes. Place in bowl and add lime or lemon juice until just covered. About 1 c will be required. Leave the fish to marinate for 2 hours in the refrigerator. Grate 2 medium size coconuts. Cut 1 lemon into wedges, 1 small onion into slices and chop 1 chilli. Combine grated coconut with above ingredients and season

*fresh ginger
(optional)*
Serves 6 to 8

with 1 t salt. Add 1 c water, stir well with hands, squeeze out the cream and strain. Strain fish and discard juice. Pour the flavoured coconut cream over the fish, garnish with grated carrot, tomato and lemon slices. Serve in chilled glass dishes. *Variation:* Add 1 T fresh chopped dill or 2 t finely chopped fresh ginger to coconut with lemon and onion.
Note: Remember that coconut cream becomes granular if it is too cold.

Kokoda with prawns

*white fish
lemon or lime juice
prawns
cucumber
kokoda sauce
dill*
Serves 6 to 8

Prepare and marinate in the refrigerator for 2 hours, 1 lb ($\frac{1}{2}$ kg) white fish as directed in basic Kokoda recipe. Cook and peel $\frac{1}{2}$ lb ($\frac{1}{4}$ kg) prawns. Cut into $\frac{1}{4}$ inch pieces. Peel and dice $\frac{1}{2}$ medium size cucumber. Drain fish and then combine with prepared prawns and cucumber. Prepare coconut sauce as directed in Basic Kokoda, adding 1 t chopped dill as additional flavouring.

Avocado with chilli tomato sauce

*avocados
lemon juice*

Cut 3 ripe but firm avocados in half and remove the stone. Sprinkle liberally with lemon juice to prevent discolouration. Chill thoroughly. Just before serving, fill cavity with the following sauce.

Sauce

*tomato
chilli sauce
sugar
spring onions
mayonnaise
salt*
Serves 6

Peel and seed 1 medium size tomato. Chop finely. Add 1 T chilli sauce, 1 t sugar, 2 T finely chopped spring onions and tomato to $\frac{1}{2}$ c mayonnaise. Season to taste with salt. Refrigerate for at least 2 hours before serving to allow full flavour to develop.

Caviar avocado

*avocados
lemon juice
salt*

Cut ripe but firm avocados in half and remove the seed. Sprinkle liberally with lemon juice to prevent discolouration and

37

garlic
caviar
parsley
Yield: as desired

then sprinkle the surface with salt and garlic juice. Finally put a large teaspoon of caviar in the centre cavity. Garnish with a sprig of parsley.
Serve well chilled on a bed of lettuce.

Moulded avocado salad
lemon jelly
water
mayonnaise
lemon juice
salt
horseradish
avocados
fresh cream
Serves 6 to 8

Dissolve 1 package of lemon jelly in 1 c boiling water. Let cool. Stir in 1 c mayonnaise, $1\frac{1}{2}$ T lemon juice, 1 t salt and $\frac{1}{4}$ t dried horseradish. Purée sufficient avocado to yield $1\frac{1}{2}$ c. Whip $\frac{1}{2}$ pint (235 ml) of fresh cream. Fold in avocado and cream and refrigerate until set.
Serve on a bed of lettuce with a slice of tomato and lime.

Apple seafood mousse
unflavoured gelatine
water
celery
cooked seafood
apple
mayonnaise
lemon juice
salt
white pepper
fresh cream
Serves 6

Soak 1 T gelatine in $\frac{1}{4}$ c cold water. Place over hot water to dissolve.
Prepare $\frac{3}{4}$ c finely chopped celery and $1\frac{1}{2}$ c cooked flaked seafood. Cut 1 medium unpeeled apple into small wedges. Mix dissolved gelatine, celery, seafood and apple together. Moisten with $\frac{1}{2}$ c mayonnaise. Season with 3 T lemon juice, 1 t salt (or to taste) and $\frac{1}{8}$ t pepper.
Fold in $\frac{1}{2}$ c whipped fresh cream. Pour into a 4 cup mould and refrigerate until set. Unmould onto a bed of water cress. Use slices of lime and chopped parsley as garnishes.
Note : Use prawns, crayfish, crab, white fish or any desired combination of seafood.

Eggplant hors d'oeuvres
eggplant
oil

Peel and cut into $\frac{1}{2}$ inch cubes $1\frac{1}{2}$–2 lb ($\frac{3}{4}$–1 kg) eggplant. Cover bottom of a heavy saucepan with oil, heat and then sauté eggplant until soft but not mushy. Drain well and place on absorbent paper until the sauce is ready.

38

Sauce

onion	Cut 1 large onion finely and crush 1 large
garlic	clove garlic. Sauté onion and garlic in 2 T
oil	oil in a heavy saucepan until soft. Stir in
tomato paste	2 T tomato paste and ½ pint (285 ml)
anchovies	tomato juice. Add 2 T chopped anchovies,
vinegar	1 T vinegar, 1 t sugar, 1 t salt and ½ c finely
sugar	chopped parsley.
salt	Simmer for 5 to 10 minutes.
parsley	Blanch 1 c finely chopped celery in boiling
celery	water for 3 minutes; drain. Stir celery and
olives or capers	eggplant into sauce.
brown bread	Serve well chilled as an appetiser garnished
butter	with freshly chopped parsley, black olives
Serves: 6	or capers on thin slices of buttered brown
	bread.

Variation : For a more substantial dish fold in 2 c cold flaked tuna.

SAUCES FOR FRUIT COCKTAILS

Avocado sauce

avocado	Sieve or blend 1 c ripe avocado. Crush ½
garlic	clove garlic and chop 2 t onion finely. Mix
onion	onion, garlic, 1 T lemon juice, 1 t salt, ½ t
lemon juice	monosodium glutamate and ¼ to 1 t chilli
salt	sauce into avocado. Beat in 1 c rich or
monosodium	evaporated milk.
glutamate	Serve well chilled with grapefruit, oranges,
chilli sauce	bananas and celery.
rich milk	
fruits	
Serves: 6	

Sweet vermouth dressing

sweet vermouth	Add ¼ c sweet vermouth, 2 T finely chopped
spring onions	spring onions and ¼ t sugar to 1 c mayon-
sugar	naise. Stir well.
mayonnaise	Serve well chilled over fruit cocktail com-
fruits	posed of equal quantities of banana and
Yield: 1¼ cups	grapefruit.

Soups

Although it may appear incongruous with the weather, soup is an important item on the menus of many hot countries. People living in India, South East Asia, the Far East and the Latin Countries have developed many delicious soup recipes.

In India, dried legumes, dhal of various kinds, are used as a basis for the thick spicy soups served with rice. In parts of the Mediterranean and South America, tomatoes flavoured with herbs, garlic and onions, often provide the background for meat, fish, and vegetable soups.

Soups from South East Asia, China and Japan are frequently made from a meat, fish or fowl stock and flavoured with ginger and soy sauce. These soups contain a variety of lightly cooked vegetables, finely cut meat or fish and occasionally egg and noodles.

The Pacific Islands are famous for their fish soups. Fish broth is seasoned with onion, chilli and salt. Rich coconut cream (lolo) is added at the last moment.

Many soups are equally good served hot or cold. For hot weather menus we have included a number which are served chilled. For example nothing could be more refreshing in the heat of the day than a bowl of chilled cucumber soup.

The success of a chilled soup depends on serving it very cold. Just a few degrees above freezing point is desirable. To achieve this, soup bowls or cups must be thoroughly cooled before the meal or arranged on a bed of crushed ice. Freeze a little of the soup mixture in an ice cube tray and put a cube or ball in each serving.

Cold soups need to be more highly seasoned than their hot counterparts, as chilling dulls the sense of taste. At the hot stage the mixture should taste a little over seasoned; when cold it will be just right.

Soups may be glamourised with colourful and tasty garnishes. These may vary from chopped crisp cucumber, thin slices of tomato, crisp bacon crumbs, toasted sesame seeds or fried cubes of bread. With a little imagination the number of garnishes may be endlessly increased. We suggest preparing a few garnishes ahead of time and storing in sealed jars in the refrigerator. For example, toasted sesame seeds and bacon crumbs.

An old fashioned meat stock is the basis of most soups. For this there is no substitute, although there are some short cuts in the stock preparation.

Stock is made by boiling meaty bones with onion, carrot, bay leaf, a bouquet of herbs and a few pepper corns. The bones should be boiled for at least 2 hours. For quicker results, they may be placed in a pressure cooker for $\frac{1}{2}$ to $\frac{3}{4}$ hour. Strain the stock, chill and skim off the fat.

A simpler method of making stock is to use stock cubes or powdered stock with the addition of vegetables and herbs.

Boil the correct proportions of stock cubes or powder and water to which some vegetables and herbs have been added. Add extra water to attain the original measurement, strain and you have a well flavoured basic stock.

During long cooking some of the stock may evaporate from the soup. Always check the volume, texture and flavour of soup before serving and add extra water, stock, milk or seasoning if necessary.

The recipes which follow are simple and delicious. The thin soups may take the place of an appetiser at dinner. The cream and thick soups do equally well as a first course or may be served in larger bowls as a lunch or supper dish.

Thin soups

Lolo fish

fish or fish heads
water
salt
onion
black pepper
chilli (optional)
thick coconut cream
lemon juice
Serves: 6

Place 2 lb (1 kg) prepared whole fish or fish heads in a saucepan. Add 7 c water, 2 t salt, 1 large onion sliced, freshly ground black pepper and 1 finely chopped chilli, if desired.

Bring slowly to simmering point and maintain until the fish is soft. Strain off stock. Add additional seasonings if required. Just before serving, stir in 2 c coconut cream and 1 T lemon juice, or to taste. Check seasoning. Serve hot, garnished with a slice of lemon.

Note: Do not boil after Coconut Cream has been added.

French onion

beef stock
onion
butter
Parmesan cheese
Serves: 6

Bring 4 c beef stock to a boil. Simmer gently.
Slice 1½ c onion finely. Fry in 3 T butter until transparent. Add to beef stock and simmer for 10 minutes.
Just before serving add 2 T Parmesan cheese.
Note: Toasted garlic croutons sprinkled on top are delicious.

Tomato mint

tomatoes
garlic
onion
oil
sweet basil (fresh)
parsley „
marjoram „
mint „
beef stock
sugar
salt
cornflour
water
Serves: 5 to 6

Chop 2 lb (1 kg) tomatoes, or use 1 lb 15 oz (1 kg) tin tomatoes. Mince 1 clove of garlic and chop 1 small onion finely. Fry onion and garlic in 1½ T of oil until golden. Add tomatoes and stir well. Season with ½ t sweet basil, 1 t finely chopped parsley, ½ t marjoram and 1 t finely chopped mint. Simmer gently for 5 minutes. Add 3 c beef stock. Add 2 t sugar and season to taste with salt. Cover and simmer for 45 minutes. Strain and thicken with 1 T cornflour mixed to a paste with 2 T water. Bring to the boil. Serve hot with a spoonful of cream and chopped spring onions, if liked.

Beef and Chinese cabbage

rump steak
cornflour
soy sauce
dry sherry
oil
water
Chinese cabbage
salt
monosodium
glutamate
Serves: 4

Slice ¼ lb (250 g) rump steak as thinly as possible. Marinate in 1 t cornflour, ½ t soy sauce, ½ t dry sherry and 2 t oil. Bring 3 c water to a boil and add 2 c shredded Chinese cabbage leaves. Return to boil and add 1 t salt and ¼ t monosodium glutamate. Cover and simmer for 10 minutes. Add meat mixture, bring to a boil, simmer for 5 minutes and serve immediately.

Cream soups

Pumpkin

butter
onion
green ginger
flour
pumpkin
chicken stock
milk
salt
Serves: 6

Melt 2 T butter in a saucepan. Add 2 T chopped onion, 1 t finely chopped green ginger ($\frac{1}{2}$ t dried ground) and sauté until transparent. Stir in 1 T flour. Add 2 c puréed cooked pumpkin and cook for 5 minutes. Gradually add 2 c chicken stock and 2 c milk. Gently simmer for 5 minutes. Season to taste with salt and rub through a sieve or purée in a blender.
Serve hot or cold, garnished with green onion or parsley.

Bhagi (Spinach)

butter
garlic
pepper
flour
chicken stock
bhagi
milk
monosodium
  glutamate
salt
Serves: 5 to 6

Melt 3 T butter in a saucepan. Add 1 large finely chopped clove of garlic. Sauté for 2 to 3 minutes. Stir in $\frac{1}{8}$ t pepper and 3 T flour. Cook and stir until a smooth paste is formed. Slowly stir in 2 c chicken stock.
Wash and remove the stems from sufficient bhagi to yield 6 oz (150 g) (roughly 1 bunch). Add bhagi to soup base, bring to a boil, cover and simmer for 5 minutes. Put through a sieve or purée in a blender. Return to stove, add 2 c milk and season with 1 t monosodium glutamate and 1 t salt, or to taste. Reheat and serve with cheese straws or flavoured crackers.

Avocado

avocado
garlic
salt
lemon juice
chilli sauce
chicken stock
milk
Serves: 6

Sieve or purée 1 cup avocado. Season with the juice from 1 clove of garlic, 1 t salt, 2 T lemon juice and $\frac{1}{2}$ t chilli sauce.
Add 1 pint (570 ml) of stock and 1 pint (570 ml) milk (or 2 pints (1·14 l) of stock) to avocado mixture and beat until a creamy consistency is reached.
Serve well chilled with a slice of lemon.
Note: May also be served hot but care

should be taken to heat gently without allowing to boil.

Cucumber

garlic
cucumber
onion
butter
flour
chicken stock
milk
salt
lemon juice
Serves: 6

Chop 1 clove garlic finely. Slice 1 cucumber, leaving the skin on. Chop 1 small onion finely. Melt 2 T butter in a saucepan. Sauté onion and garlic until clear. Add cucumber, reserving a little for garnish. Sauté for 5 minutes more. Stir in 2 T flour and cook for 1 minute. Slowly stir in 2 c chicken stock. Cook until cucumber is tender. Purée by putting through a sieve or blender. Return to stove, reheat and add 2 c milk. Season with 1 t salt and $\frac{1}{2}$ t lemon juice. Serve with small triangles of cucumber floating on surface of soup.
Variation: Serve well chilled with whipped cream.
Note: Soup should be a pale green colour. To achieve this use a dark green cucumber or add a few spinach leaves or a few drops of green food colouring.

Thick soups

Eggplant

onion
bacon
garlic
coriander seeds
oil
eggplant
beef stock
parsley
Serves: 5 to 6

Finely chop 1 medium size onion, 1 large rasher of bacon (2 oz) (50 g) and 1 clove of garlic. Sauté onion, bacon, garlic and 2 level t whole coriander seeds in 2 T oil for 3 to 4 minutes. Peel and slice 4 medium size eggplant (1 lb or $\frac{1}{2}$ kg). Add to onion mixture and cook for a further 5 minutes. Add 4 c beef stock, cover and simmer for 1 hour. Skim off any excess fat. Put through a sieve or purée in a blender. Adjust seasoning and reheat.
Serve hot with finely chopped parsley as a garnish.

Dhal

dhal (split peas)
water
salt
turmeric
onion
garlic
ghee or butter
cumin seed
salt
pepper
coriander or parsley
Serves: 6

Wash 2 c split peas and put in saucepan with 5 c water, 1 t salt, 1 t turmeric and $\frac{1}{2}$ medium size onion sliced. Simmer until peas are soft. Finely chop remaining $\frac{1}{2}$ onion. Crush 1 clove of garlic. Heat 2 T ghee or butter in saucepan and sauté onion and garlic. Add $\frac{1}{4}$ t of cumin seed and sauté for 3 to 4 minutes. Combine split peas with onion, garlic and cumin. Simmer for 10 minutes. Season to taste with salt and pepper. Serve garnished with chopped green coriander leaves or parsley.

Tropical vegetable

onions
oil
potatoes, taro
  or yam
tomatoes
watercress or
  spinach
mint
water
salt
green beans, long or
  French beans
celery
Chinese marrow
  or cucumber
parsley
Serves: 6

Chop 1 medium size onion and fry in 2 T hot oil in saucepan until golden. Add 1 c diced potato, taro or yam, 4 medium size tomatoes peeled and chopped, 1 bunch chopped watercress or spinach and 1 sprig of mint. Stir fry for 3 minutes. Add 5 c water and $1\frac{1}{2}$ t salt. Simmer until tender. Add $1\frac{1}{2}$ c sliced long or French beans, 2 stalks of celery finely chopped and 1 c of finely chopped Chinese marrow or cucumber. Simmer until just tender. Finely chop 1 bunch of parsley. Add to soup just before serving.
This thick soup is excellent served with cheese for supper.

Red beet

beetroot
onion
celery
beef stock
salt, pepper
tomatoes or
  tomato paste

Chop finely 12 oz (300 g) canned beetroot, 1 medium size onion and 2 stalks of celery. Heat 5 c beef stock in a saucepan. Stir in prepared vegetables and season to taste with salt and pepper. Cook until celery is soft. Add 2 medium chopped tomatoes or 1 T tomato paste. Simmer for 5 minutes or

lemon juice
vinegar
sugar
egg yolks
Serves: 6

until tomato is mushy. Rub stock through a sieve or purée in a blender.

Season soup with 3 T lemon juice, 1 T vinegar and 1 T sugar.

Adjust seasoning for salt and pepper.

Bring soup to the boil. Slowly pour soup over 2 well beaten egg yolks in a bowl. Beat well. Chill the soup thoroughly.

Serve with sour cream flavoured with chives. Whipped cream may be used as a substitute for the sour cream if desired.

Kai

A famous soup made from fresh water shellfish.

Fresh kais should be kept in a bucket of water for at least one day before using, to remove river sand. Kais will stay alive in fresh water for four to five days but the water must be changed daily.

kai
water
butter
onion
chilli
flour
milk
salt
pepper
lemon
Serves: 6

Scrub 10 to 15 kais (depending on the size), place in a saucepan and cover with boiling water. Simmer until the shells open. Remove the flesh from the shells. Cut away the hard white "beard" and discard.

Mince the kais, or place in a blender with some of the liquor from the saucepan. Add further liquor until a thin mixture is achieved. Bring this to a boil and then strain to remove any tough pieces of muscle. Measure mixture and then add sufficient liquor to yield 4 c.

Melt 5 T butter in a saucepan. Add 2 T finely chopped onion and $\frac{1}{2}$ t finely chopped chilli. Sauté until golden. Stir in 5 T flour to form a smooth paste. Slowly add 1 c milk and kai mixture. Simmer for 5 minutes. Season to taste with salt and pepper.

Just before serving add 2 T lemon juice. Garnish with chopped chives or parsley and a thin slice of lemon.

Salads and Dressings

POMELO

MANDARIN

GRAPEFRUIT

LEMON

COMQUAT

ORANGE

LIME

WILD LEMON

DALO

BREADFRUIT

A cold salad is an ideal dish for the tropical menu. In many hot countries salads are not served frequently because the traditional lettuce, cress and celery are not available.

Raw salad vegetables which may be found in most hot climate markets are green peppers (capsicums), white radishes, Chinese cabbage, water cress, spring onions, bean sprouts and tomatoes. For those who have a garden, we suggest putting aside a small area for growing salad vegetables together with a few herbs such as parsley, chives, mint and basil.

A number of tropical vegetables and fruits are delicious cooked and served as salad. Sometimes a cooked vegetable may be combined with a raw fruit as in Tropical Bean Salad or Spiced Kumala and Banana Salad.

The success of a salad depends on the dressing that accompanies it. It is a good idea to keep one or two basic dressings in a bottle in the refrigerator. Flavourings may then be added to suit the salad of the day.

Dressings

Basic Egg

egg yolk
salt
cayenne pepper
dry mustard
sugar
vinegar
salad oil
Yield: $1\frac{1}{4}$ cups

MAYONNAISE

Beat 1 egg yolk in a mixing bowl with $\frac{1}{2}$ t salt, few grains of cayenne pepper, $\frac{1}{2}$ t dry mustard and $\frac{1}{2}$ t sugar. Add 1 T white or malt vinegar and continue beating. Slowly add 1 c salad oil drop by drop, being sure to blend thoroughly as you do so. Thin to desired consistency with a further $\frac{1}{2}$ or 1 T vinegar after the mixture has thickened. Store in a covered jar in the refrigerator. *Variation:* Substitute 2 T lime or lemon juice for the vinegar in the standard recipe. This does not keep as well but is excellent if it is to be used within one or two days.

Russian dressing

egg
tomato sauce
green pepper
chilli sauce
mayonnaise
Yield: 1½ cups

Fold 1 finely chopped hard-boiled egg, 2 T tomato sauce (ketchup), 2 T chopped green pepper and 1 T chilli sauce into 1 c mayonnaise.
Serve with tossed green salad; as a dressing for potato salad; or in a fish or seafood salad.

Cole slaw dressing

mayonnaise
lemon juice
caster sugar
Yield: 1¼ cups

Mix ½ c mayonnaise, ½ c lemon juice and ¼ c caster sugar together. Place in a screw-topped jar and refrigerate.
To serve, mix with finely shredded cabbage.

FRENCH DRESSINGS

Basic French

garlic
salt
black pepper
sugar
vinegar or lemon juice
salad oil
Yield: 1 cup

Crush 1 small clove garlic in 1 t salt. Add a dash of black pepper and 1 t sugar. Beat in ¼ c lemon juice or vinegar and then ¾ c salad oil.
Store in a bottle and shake well before using.

Variations
Yield: ½ cup

Fresh Herb Dressing. Add 1 T finely chopped fresh herbs to ½ c French dressing just before serving.

Yield: 1 cup

Curry Dressing. Add 1 t curry powder to 1 c French dressing.

Yield: 1 cup

Tomato Dressing. Use tomato purée and 2 T lemon juice in the basic French dressing recipe, in place of all lemon juice.

Blue cheese dressing

blue cheese
cream cheese
Parmesan cheese
garlic salt

Mash 2 oz (50 g) blue cheese with a fork. Beat in 4 oz (100 g) softened cream cheese and 1 T Parmesan cheese. Season with ½ t garlic salt and ¼ t tarragon.

tarragon (dried)	Add ½ c milk, 1 T at a time; beating well
milk	after each addition.
Yield: 1 cup	

Pawpaw seed dressing

sugar	Place ¼ c sugar, ½ t salt, ½ t dry mustard,
salt	½ c malt vinegar, 1 c salad oil, 2 T minced
dry mustard	onion and 1 T pawpaw seed in the blender.
malt vinegar	Blend until a smooth creamy dressing is
salad oil	achieved.
onion	Serve as a sauce for fish cocktail (pink
pawpaw seed	salmon with banana, celery and apple on a
Yield: 2 cups	bed of lettuce), or a fruit cocktail with equal
	quantities of banana, pawpaw and apple.

Sesame oil dressing

salad oil	Put ⅓ c salad oil and ⅓ c sesame oil in a bowl.
sesame oil	Add 2 t soy sauce, 1 t prepared mustard, ¼ t
soy sauce	black pepper and ⅓ c lemon juice. Beat
prepared mustard	thoroughly.
black pepper	This dressing is excellent for rice, bean-
lemon juice	sprout or Chinese cabbage salads.
Yield: 1 cup	

Banana radish dressing

bananas	Mash 2 bananas or sufficient to yield 1 c
white radish	pulp. Grate 2 T fresh white radish.
mayonnaise	Blend bananas, radish and ¼ c mayonnaise.
lemon juice	Season with 1 T lemon juice, ¼ t salt, 1 t
salt	caster sugar and ¼ t Worcestershire sauce.
caster sugar	Excellent served with cabbage slaw.
Worcestershire sauce	
Yield: 1½ cups	

Gelatine salads

Gelatine salads may be made from prepared packeted aspic or from gelatine in combination with fruit juice or stock.

If possible, refrigerate for at least 12 hours before serving.

You may have suitable moulds on hand or any number of substitutes may be used. For example a small tin from fish or reduced cream may be used for an individual mould. A plain bowl or a cake tin is quite suitable for a large salad.

Unmoulding : Make sure your jelly is well set, by making it the day before you desire to use it if possible. Remove jelly from the refrigerator and turn upside down on to serving platter. Cover the bowl with a hot wet cloth so the jelly will melt around the outside and the bowl will slip off. This just takes a moment, so be careful not to overdo it. Put jelly back in refrigerator immediately to refirm. Remove one hour later to garnish with lettuce, carrot curls, olives, etc. as you prefer. Return to refrigerator and do not remove again until ready to serve.

If a square cake-tin is used, cut the jelly in squares with a knife and remove to a dish using a knife and lifter. This is a particularly easy and attractive way of achieving uniform shapes if time is short or you are serving large numbers.

Tomato aspic

gelatine
water
bay leaf
oregano (dried)
sugar
tomato juice
salt
Worcestershire
  sauce
lemon juice
celery or cucumber
Serves: 6

Mix 1 envelope or 3 t gelatine with $\frac{1}{2}$ c water. Add 1 bay leaf, $\frac{1}{4}$ t dried oregano (optional), 2 t sugar and bring just to a boil. Strain and add $1\frac{3}{4}$ c tomato juice. Add $\frac{1}{4}$ t salt, $\frac{1}{4}$ t Worcestershire sauce, 1 t lemon juice. Chill until partially set.
Fold in $\frac{1}{2}$ c finely chopped celery or cucumber.
Serve over lettuce or finely shredded Chinese cabbage.
This may be served as a first course or as part of a salad accompanying cold meat.

Tomato aspic with seafood

crayfish or crab
tomato aspic
lettuce or cress
Serves: 6

A delicious variation of Tomato Aspic. Reduce celery or cucumber to $\frac{1}{4}$ c and add $\frac{1}{2}$ c fresh cooked flaked crayfish or crab. Pour into individual moulds. Unmould onto lettuce leaves or cress and garnish with a sprig of parsley and a spoon of mayonnaise. Teacups may be used quite satisfactorily if gelatine moulds are not available.

Chicken aspic

Season 2 c chicken stock to taste with salt

52

and pepper. (If chicken stock is bland, we suggest bringing it to a boil and simmering with 1 T chopped parsley, ¼ c each of chopped onion, carrot and celery and ½ t thyme. Strain.)

chicken stock
salt, pepper
gelatine
celery
carrot
green pepper
cooked chicken
lettuce
Serves: 6

Soak 1 T gelatine in ¼ c cold water for 5 minutes. Stir into hot stock till dissolved. Chill. When partially set, fold in ½ c finely chopped celery, ½ c finely grated carrot, 2 T chopped green pepper and 2 c cubed cooked chicken. Place in an 8 inch square cake tin and refrigerate until firm; preferably the next day.

Serve on a bed of lettuce with other salad accompaniments; garnish with a wedge of tomato and a sprig of parsley.

Pea, pickle, celery

lemon jelly
water
lemon juice
celery
gherkins
peas
Serves: 5 to 6

Dissolve 1 package lemon jelly in 2 c boiling water. Add 2 T lemon juice. Refrigerate until partially set. Fold in ½ c finely chopped celery, ¼ c chopped sweet gherkins and 1 c cooked peas. Chill until firm.

This tangy refreshing salad is delicious with fish or meat or just by itself.

Rou rou (taro leaves) salad

rou rou (taro leaves)
coconut cream
salt
onion
gelatine
water
Serves: 6

Prepare 1 lb (½ kg) young taro leaves. Remove stalks. Make 2 c coconut cream, bring to boil and add 1 t salt and ½ medium sized onion, finely chopped. Add the leaves, boil for 5 minutes, turn over and boil for a further 5 minutes.

Soak 1 T gelatine in ¼ c cold water. Stir into cooked taro leaves. Mash up leaves with a fork. Pour mixture into a shallow dish or into a mould and refrigerate until set.

Variations: Prawn Salad

Add 1 c prepared cooked prawns to the mixture.

Tomato

Line the mould with tomato slices or fill a

mould with alternate layers of tomatoes and
rou rou.

Lumi (Seaweed Salad)

lumi (seaweed)
coconut cream
onion
salt
monosodium
  glutamate
green colouring
Serves: 6

Place $\frac{1}{2}$ lb ($\frac{1}{4}$ kg) thoroughly washed lumi in
a saucepan with $2\frac{1}{2}$ c coconut cream. Add 1
medium onion finely chopped, $1\frac{1}{2}$ t salt
and $\frac{1}{2}$ t monosodium glutamate. Heat and
cook until mixture is thick. Most of the lumi
will dissolve. Add a little green colouring.
Pour into a flat dish or mould and
refrigerate.
Variations: Add raw tomato or spring
onions.

Substantial salads

Many of the starchy roots and fruits which grow in tropical
countries can be used as a base for the more substantial type of
salad.
Nearly all of these foods have a much better flavour if cooked in
the skin. Prepared as directed, they form the basis of particularly
good salads and may be used to replace potato in recipes.
Steam, boil or bake the root or fruit, remove the skin and then
dice or cut into $\frac{1}{4}$–$\frac{1}{2}$ inch cubes or into slices.
For further information on unfamiliar vegetables, refer to the
chart, p. 158.

Breadfruit

Puncture a breadfruit with a skewer in
several places. Put in the oven at 350° F
and bake about 1 hour. Test with a skewer
to see if soft.

Kumala (sweet potato)

Scrub well and then steam or boil until soft.
When cool remove skins.

Taro

Peel first and then steam or boil until soft.

Yam

Bake or steam in the skin or peel and boil.

54

Vudi (cooking banana)

Boil or steam and then peel.

Spiced kumala (sweet potato) and banana salad

kumala
banana
lemon juice
oil
curry powder
garlic
mayonnaise
spring onions
coriander or parsley
Serves: 8

Cut 1 lb ($\frac{1}{2}$ kg) cooked kumala into cubes. Slice 4 ripe bananas and marinate in $\frac{1}{4}$ c lemon juice. Heat 2 T oil in a saucepan. Sauté 2 t curry powder and 2 crushed cloves garlic. Cool and combine with $\frac{1}{2}$ c mayonnaise.
Combine kumala and banana. Fold in curry dressing and $\frac{1}{4}$ c chopped spring onions. Garnish with chopped parsley or coriander leaves.

Tafolu prawn salad

breadfruit
coconut cream
cornflour
onion
lemon juice
celery or cucumber
prawns
salt
chilli
Serves: 6

Bake a breadfruit in the oven, or if possible, in the ashes. A fruit cooked in the fire has a particularly good flavour. (Always puncture fruit with a skewer before baking.) Prepare 4 c coconut cream.
Peel the baked breadfruit. Place the soft flesh in a large bowl and pound until smooth with a heavy spoon, a clean stone or with the hands. Work in coconut cream until a pastry like consistency is achieved. Cut into cubes or roll in balls. Place remaining cream in a saucepan with 2 t cornflour for each cup of cream. Bring to the boiling point stirring constantly till thick—simmer but do not boil. Season the thickened cream with 1 T finely chopped onion, $\frac{1}{3}$ c lemon juice, $\frac{3}{4}$ c diced cucumber or chopped celery, 1 c cooked prawns, salt and chilli to taste.
Combine the prawn cream with the breadfruit. Refrigerate for several hours before serving. Garnish with parsley and lemon slices.

Hot rice salad

rice
eggs
capers
mayonnaise
caraway seed
salt
pepper
cream crackers
Serves: 6

Prepare 3 c boiled rice and 2 hard-boiled eggs. Chop eggs and 2 T capers finely. Toss rice, egg and capers together. Add ½ c mayonnaise or sufficient to moisten thoroughly. Season with ½ t caraway seed, salt and pepper to taste.
Keep hot until ready to serve. Gently fold in 1 c coarsely crumbled soda crackers (cream crackers).
Serve immediately with corned beef or ham.
Note: Do not add crackers until the last moment or they will go soggy. If caraway seeds are not available fennel may be substituted.

Spring onion and potato salad

potatoes
eggs
spring onions
mayonnaise
dry mustard
cayenne pepper
salt
pepper
Serves: 6

Cook, peel and cube sufficient potatoes to yield 3 c. Boil, peel and chop 4 eggs, reserving centre slices as a garnish. Prepare ½ c finely chopped spring onion.
Mix together potato, egg and onion. Add ½ c mayonnaise or sufficient to moisten to the desired consistency. Season with ½ t dry mustard, ¼ t cayenne pepper, salt and pepper to taste. Chill.
Serve garnished with egg slices and sprigs of parsley.

Sweet and sour eggplant (baigan)

eggplant (baigan)
water
salad oil
coriander seed
salt
lemon juice or vinegar
herbs, fresh
bay leaf
currants
Serves: 6

Peel and dice 4 large eggplant into ½ inch cubes.
Put 2½ c water, ¼ c salad oil, ½ t crushed coriander seed, 1 t salt, ½ c lemon juice or white vinegar, a bunch of fresh herbs and a bay leaf into a saucepan. Bring to a boil. Add eggplant and simmer until just tender (must not be mushy). Remove eggplant and reduce liquor by half, through boiling. Strain. Add ½ c currants. Simmer for 5 minutes. Pour over cooked eggplant and chill.

Serve with lemon slices and chopped parsley.

Tropical bean salad

tinned kidney beans
pineapple
green pepper
long beans
butter beans
tomato
salt
pepper
French dressing
Serves: 4 to 6

Mix 1 lb ($\frac{1}{2}$ kg) tin of drained and washed kidney beans with 3 slices of finely sliced pineapple (fresh or tinned). Add $\frac{1}{4}$ c finely chopped green pepper. Cook, cool and add $\frac{1}{2}$ c each of cooked, cooled young long beans and butter beans. Section and remove the seeds from 1 large tomato. Cut into fine strips. Add to salad. Fold in 2 T French Dressing. Season to taste with salt and pepper.
Perfect with cold meat and looks very attractive on a buffet table.

Long bean salad

long beans
French dressing
sweet basil
Serves: 6

Wash, cut and cook until just tender (3 to 4 minutes) 2 c long beans. Drain and chill thoroughly. Toss in French Dressing, sprinkle with $\frac{1}{4}$ t dried basil and serve after a further 20 minutes in the refrigerator.
Variation: Fresh Herb Dressing, Curry Dressing or Tomato Dressing may be substituted. French beans may be substituted for long beans.

Bean sprouts

Bean sprouts may be obtained from any market that supplies Chinese food. These make delicious crisp salads and have the added advantage of a high nutritive value. We recommend bean sprouts as a useful addition to tropical salads which often lack crispness. Bean sprouts may be grown at home, see below.

How to grow bean sprouts

Put a piece of sacking or any other thick coarse material in the bottom of shallow dish. Saturate with water. Sprinkle with

57

green mung seed. This is obtainable at Chinese or Indian grocery shops. Put the dish in a dark place and keep moist. The sprouts will be ready in 3-4 days time, when 1½-2 inches in length. Wash well, remove seeds.

Bean sprout salad

bean sprouts
carrot
spring onion
sesame dressing
Serves: 6

Wash about 2-3 c bean sprouts and place on a towel to dry. Put in a bowl and add ½ c grated carrot and ½ c chopped spring onion. Toss with Sesame Dressing. Serve on lettuce leaves or plain.

Sprouted dried pea salad

blue peas, dried
water
salt
mint
French dressing
Serves: 6

Put 1½ c dried blue peas in a bowl, cover with water and leave for one day. Drain off water and keep very moist in a cool place for another day, or long enough for peas to germinate and produce sprouts ¼ inch long. Peas ferment very easily in hot weather and it is therefore wise to put into the refrigerator during the second day. Cover the dish to retain moisture. Place sprouted peas in boiling water with salt and a sprig of mint. Boil until tender. Remove loose skins. Toss with French Dressing and garnish with mint leaves just before serving.

Chinese cabbage and carrot salad

Chinese cabbage
raw carrot
blue cheese dressing
Serves: 6

Shred sufficient Chinese cabbage finely to yield 1½ c, and grate 1½ c raw carrot. Toss together. Place ½ c salad on each plate with 2 T Blue Cheese Dressing on top.

Ota salad

ota, well curled
water
salt
miti or French
  dressing

Select a bunch of very young, well curled ota fern (frond stage). Cut off the top 4 to 5 inches of crisp stalk. With a sharp knife, split the stalks into four. Place in boiling salty water and cook for 2 minutes, turn

58

Serves: as desired

over and cook another 2 minutes. Ota must be very crisp, do not overcook. Drain well and cool.
Serve with French Dressing or Miti.

Baseisei

rou rou (taro) stalks
water
salt
lemon juice or miti
onion
Serves: as desired

Select light green young stalks of rou rou. Remove the leaves or use pink or green thick stems of the root from which the leaves have been removed. Carefully strip off the outer skin. Cut into 4 inch pieces, tie into bundles and place in boiling salted water. Boil a few minutes until just tender. Remove and drain. With a sharp knife or a fork shred the stems. Just before serving add lemon juice or Miti to just cover the shredded stems, and a little finely chopped onion.

Main dish salads

Kora banana ota

kora
onion
butter
water
ota
salt
coconut cream
tomato
banana
paprika
Serves: 6

Press 1 c prepared Kora (p. 36) into a large cup and refrigerate.
Fry 1 c coarsely chopped onion in 2 T butter mixed with ¼ c water until the water has evaporated and the onion is a pale golden colour. Cook sufficient ota to yield 2 c. Simmer in boiling salted water until just tender (3 to 4 minutes). Drain, rinse in cold water and then redrain well.
Prepare 1 c coconut cream. Mix with onion and ota. Refrigerate for 2 hours. Cut 1 large tomato into quarters. Remove the seeds. Cut the flesh into thin strips (julienne). Have a large flat serving dish on hand, invert chilled Kora into centre of dish. Drain excess coconut cream off ota and arrange ota around Kora. Arrange tomato strips attractively on top of ota. Finally just before serving, peel and cut 3

59

medium size bananas diagonally and arrange around outside of dish.

A dash of paprika on top of Kora, and a delicious and attractive salad is ready to be served. Excellent in combination with well-chilled meat or tinned sockeye salmon.

Potato and sausage salad

potatoes
peas
pork sausages
tomato
parsley
French dressing
basil
salt
pepper
Serves: 4 to 6

Peel, cube and cook sufficient potatoes to yield 2 c. Cook ¾ c frozen or fresh peas. Fry or grill 4 pork sausages until golden and cooked thoroughly. Chill. Peel, seed and slice 1 large tomato. Finely chop 1 T parsley. Combine hot potato and peas with 6 to 8 T French Dressing. Season with ¼ t basil, salt and pepper to taste. Slice cold sausages. Carefully toss sausage, tomato and parsley into salad. Recheck seasonings, chill until ready to serve.

Prawn rice salad

prawns
rice
celery or cucumber
bacon
mandarin oranges
coconut, freshly
  grated
sour cream
monosodium
  glutamate
lemon juice
salt
pepper
Serves: 6

Cook and peel 2 dozen large prawns. Cut in thirds. Prepare 4 c cooked rice. Coarsely chop 1 c cucumber or celery. Finely chop 2 rashers bacon and fry until golden. Drain 1 small tin (8 oz or ¼ kg) mandarin oranges. Mix prawns, rice, celery, mandarin orange, bacon and ¼ c freshly grated coconut together. Moisten with ½ c sour cream, flavoured with ¼ t monosodium glutamate and 2 t lemon juice. Season to taste with salt and pepper.

Serve well chilled on a bed of water cress.

Note: Fresh mandarin orange may be substituted for tinned, with the addition of sugar.

Cheesey bean salad

cheese
apples
lemon juice

Cube ½ lb (¼ kg) cheese. Core and finely chop 2 medium unpeeled red apples. Place in a bowl with 2 T lemon juice. Chop

60

celery
long beans
mayonnaise
sugar
salt
black pepper
Serves: 6

celery finely to yield 1 c. Slice sufficient long beans to yield 2 c. Cook 5 minutes or until tender but still crisp. Chill.

Toss beans, cheese, apple and celery together. Add $\frac{1}{4}$ c mayonnaise or sufficient to reach the desired consistency. Season with 2 t sugar, salt and freshly ground black pepper.

Variations: Add $\frac{1}{4}$ c coarsely chopped black olives. French beans may be substituted for long beans.

NAMES OF SOME FRUITS AND VEGETABLES COMMONLY FOUND IN THE TROPICS

Common Name	Botanical Name
Avocado pear Alligator pear Soldires Butter	Persea gratissima
Banana Plantain	Musa sapientum
Brazilian Cherry Lovi lovi Tomi-tomi	Flacourtia inermis
Breadfruit	Artocarpus incisa
Cassava Tapioca Manioc	Manihot utilissima
Chilli	Capsicum frutescens
Chinese Cabbage China Cabbage Shantung Cabbage	Brassica chinensis

61

Common Name	Botanical Name
Chinese Marrow	Cucumis sativus var
Duruka Pitpit	Erienthus maximus
Eggplant Aubergine Brinjal	Solanum Melongena
Guava	Psidium Guyava
Grapefruit	Citrus grandis
Green peppers Sweet peppers Capsicum Bele pepper	Capsicum grossum
Indian Cherry Surinam Cherry	Eugenia Michelii
Mango	Mangifera indica
Okra Gumbo Lady's fingers	Hibiscus esculentus
Ota	Athyrium esculentus
Passion fruit Sweet Cup	Passiflora edulis
Paw paw Papaya Papeta Tree melon Mummy Apple	Carica Papaya

Common Name	Botanical Name
Radish (white)	Raphanus sativus (fam. Cruciferae)
Rockmelon Musk Melon Cantaloupe	Cucumis Melo
Rosella Roselle Tamaca Sorrel Red Sorrel Rou rou	Hibiscus sabariffa
Taro leaves Dalo leaves	Colocasia Antiquorum
Sour Sop	Anona muricata
Sweet Potato	Ipomea Batatas
Water Melon	Citrullus vulgaris (fam. Cucurbitaceae)

The Main Course

Menu specialities— something hot and different
SOUFFLES

Basic cheese soufflé

butter
flour
dry mustard
salt
milk
cheese
eggs
Serves: 3 to 4

Melt 4 T butter in a saucepan. Mix 4 T flour, 1 t salt and 1 t mustard together. Stir into melted butter to form a smooth paste. Slowly add 1 c milk whilst stirring constantly over low heat. When thick and smooth, remove from stove and stir in 1 c finely grated Cheddar cheese. Separate 4 eggs. Beat egg whites until stiff but not dry. Using the same beaters beat egg yolks until stiff and creamy. Blend egg yolks into sauce. Fold egg whites into sauce, mixing only until there are no large areas of sauce remaining. Pour into a greased straight-sided 3 pt dish and bake at 350° F in a shallow pan of hot water for 40 to 50 minutes. It will have risen and be dry and golden brown in colour when done.
Serve immediately.
Variations: Spring Onion Soufflé
Proceed as directed in standard soufflé but

67

stir $\frac{1}{2}$ c finely chopped spring onions into sauce before folding into egg whites.

Fish Soufflé

Proceed as in standard recipe but fold in $\frac{3}{4}$ c flaked cooked or tinned fish, seasoned to taste with salt, into sauce. Reduce cheese to $\frac{1}{2}$ c.

Rou Rou Soufflé

Proceed as in standard recipe but fold $\frac{1}{2}$ c cooked chopped rou rou into sauce.

Lolo fish soufflé

butter
flour
salt
chilli sauce
coconut cream
fish
onion
eggs
Serves: 4

Melt 4 T butter in a saucepan. Mix 4 T flour, 1 t salt and 1 t chilli sauce together. Stir in melted butter to form a smooth paste. Slowly add 1 c coconut cream whilst stirring constantly over low heat. When thick and smooth, remove from heat. Flake sufficient cooked fish to make 1 c. Fry $\frac{1}{2}$ c finely chopped onion in butter until golden. Fold fish and onion into sauce. Separate 4 eggs. Beat egg whites until stiff but not dry. Using the same beaters, beat egg yolks until stiff and creamy. Blend egg yolks into sauce. Fold egg whites into sauce, mixing only until there are no large areas of sauce remaining.
Bake as directed in Basic Cheese Soufflé.
Variation: Add 2 t lemon juice and a little grated lemon rind to cooked fish.

Egg foo yung

bean sprouts, fresh
green pepper
spring onions
oil
ham, prawns or pork
eggs
water
salt

Wash well $\frac{1}{2}$ lb (200 g) fresh bean sprouts. Finely chop 1 green pepper and 4 spring onions. Fry bean sprouts and green pepper in 4 T oil for 5 minutes, stirring frequently. Drain and put aside. Dice sufficient cooked ham, prawns or pork to yield 1 c. Beat 8 eggs well. Add $\frac{1}{2}$ c water, 1 t salt, and $\frac{1}{2}$ t monosodium glutamate. Stir in vegetables

68

monosodium
glutamate
Serves: 6

and meat or prawns. Pour 1/6 mixture at a time into hot lightly oiled fry pan. Tilt pan to cover evenly. Let cook until brown underneath and surface is dry. Fold in half. Cook 1 minute more. Serve with the following Soy Sauce Broth.

Soy sauce broth

soy sauce
sugar
vinegar
chicken stock
Yield: 1½ cups

Bring ¼ c soy sauce, 2 T sugar, 2 T vinegar and 1 c chicken stock to a boil. Reduce heat and keep warm until ready to serve.

Fried rice

rice
spring onions
Chinese mushrooms
prawns
pork
salt
pepper (optional)
sherry
soy sauce
hoisin sauce
  (optional)
oil
eggs
monosodium
glutamate
Serves: 6 to 8

Prepare 4 c cooked rice. Finely chop ½ c spring onions. Soak 4 large Chinese dried mushrooms in boiling water for 20 minutes. Squeeze dry, remove stems and thinly slice. Chop 1 dozen cooked prawns into bite size pieces. Cut ½ lb (¼ kg) pork into ½ inch cubes. Prepare a marinade of ¼ t salt, ⅛ t pepper, 2 t sherry, 1 T soy sauce and 1 T hoisin sauce. Marinate meat for 2 hours (optional). Heat 1 T oil in a fry pan until hot. Beat 3 eggs. Pour ½ mixture in pan and leave until set. Turn and remove from pan. Repeat with other half of egg mixture. Dice cooked egg and put aside. Heat 6 T oil in fry pan until very hot. Fry drained marinated pork until done. Add spring onions, mushrooms and prawns. Stir fry for 2 to 3 minutes. Stir in rice, tossing to mix and coat evenly. Season with 1 t salt, ¼ t pepper, 1 T soy sauce and ½ t monosodium glutamate. Toss in chopped egg and stir fry for 5 minutes.
Variations: Cooked chicken, bacon, pork or beef may be substituted for marinated pork. Prawns may be omitted.

69

Pilau

long grain rice
garlic
onion
ghee or butter
cloves
peppercorns
cinnamon stick
cardamom pods
turmeric
salt
water or stock
chicken or lamb
almonds
raisins
Serves: 6

Wash 1½ c rice and drain until dry. Crush 1 clove garlic and finely chop one small onion. Heat 2 T butter or ghee in a saucepan and sauté garlic and onion. Bruise 3 cloves, 4 to 6 peppercorns, 1½ inch piece of cinnamon and 2 cardamoms with a rolling pin or wooden spoon. Add these and 1 t turmeric to onions. Sauté for a few minutes. Add 1½ c rice. Cook, stirring constantly, for about 5 minutes. Add 3 c stock (or water) and 1 t salt. Boil for 5 minutes and add 1 c finely chopped cooked chicken or lamb.
Place close-fitting lid on saucepan and put in oven at 250° F for 20 to 30 minutes. Take out and stir with a fork to give dry fluffy appearance to rice. Sauté 8–12 peeled (blanched) and halved almonds until golden brown in 1 T butter. Remove from stove and add ¼ c raisins. Top pilau with browned raisins and almonds and serve with Raita.

Raita

cucumber
tomatoes
potatoes
onion
yoghurt (dehi)
salt
Yield: 5 to 6 cups

Peel and cube ½ medium cucumber, put in a strainer and drain off juice which forms. Add 2 medium size cooked, cubed potatoes. Finely chop ½ small onion and 2–3 tomatoes. Toss together with 2 c yoghurt and season with ½ t salt.
There are many variations which you may make with raita. A few are given below. Serve with pilau or curry.
Variations: Substitute taro, tapioca or yam for potato. Green peppers may be used instead of or as well as cucumber. Celery may be substituted for cucumber.
Add 2 T finely chopped parsley or coriander leaves.
Add 2 T finely chopped spring onion instead of dry onion.

Cheese and bacon puff

bacon
bread
cheese
egg
milk
salt
pepper
dry mustard
Serves: 6

Chop and fry 4 rashers of bacon until golden. Remove bacon and put aside. Prepare 4 sandwiches (8 slices bread) spreading bacon fat on the inside instead of butter and fill with sliced cheese. Cut into quarters diagonally. Beat 2 eggs with 2 c milk. Add ½ t salt, ¼ t pepper and 1 t dry mustard.

Place sandwiches in casserole dish with points upwards. Sprinkle with bacon. Pour egg-milk mixture over carefully.

Place casserole dish in a shallow pan of hot water. Bake in a moderate (350° F) oven for 1 hour or until puffy and golden.

Rou rou quiche Lorraine

eggs
evaporated milk
cheese
onion
rou rou
crab meat
salt
cayenne pepper
short crust pastry
Serves: 4 to 6

Beat 2 eggs with ¾ c evaporated milk. Add 1 c finely grated cheese (4 oz or 100 g), 1 T grated onion, ¾ c cooked chopped rou rou and 1 c cooked crab meat. Season with 1 t salt, and ¼ t cayenne pepper. Carefully pour into 9 inch unbaked pie shell of Short Crust Pastry (page 144).

Bake in 425° F oven for the first 10 minutes, reduce heat to 325° F and bake for 25 to 30 minutes more. It will be firm and slightly puffy when done.

Serve immediately. A delicious lunch or supper dish.

Coconut and egg curry

coconut
lemon juice
onion
butter or ghee
turmeric
ground coriander
   dried
chilli powder

Crack one coconut and reserve the water. Grate the flesh and mix with 1 T lemon juice. Thinly slice 4 large onions. Pulverize ¼ c onion slices with a wooden spoon. Fry pulverised onion in 3 T ghee or butter. Add 1 t turmeric, 1 t coriander, ½ to 1 t chilli powder and stir fry for 1 minute. Add the grated coconut and cook 5 minutes. Add

71

salt
eggs
Serves: 4 to 5

sliced onions and coconut water and simmer until cooked. Season with salt. Slice
6 hard boiled eggs and place in a flat dish.
Cover with sauce and keep hot for 10
minutes before serving to allow flavour to
penetrate.

Pizza

Dough

yeast
water
salad oil
salt
flour

Place 2 T dried yeast in $\frac{1}{2}$ c lukewarm
water. Leave to react for 10 minutes. Add a
further $1\frac{1}{2}$ c warm water, $\frac{1}{4}$ c salad oil, $1\frac{1}{2}$ t
salt and stir well. Measure and sift 6 c flour.
Beat in 3 c flour or enough to form a stiff
batter. Work in the remaining flour until a
soft non-sticky dough is formed. Place on a
floured board and knead thoroughly, dusting with more flour when necessary. When
a smooth springy dough is achieved with
small air bubbles on the surface, it has been
kneaded sufficiently. Place dough in a
greased bowl, oil the top, cover with a damp
cloth and leave to rise until it has doubled
in bulk and a depression made with the
finger remains.
Punch down dough, and then divide into 4
equal pieces. Roll out on a slightly oiled
board until a size slightly larger than the pie
tray is achieved. Ease onto greased trays
(say 4 10-inch trays). Trim edges with a
knife. Add topping as directed below.

Sauce

garlic
onion
salad oil
mince (beef)
tinned tomatoes
tomato paste
oregano

Sauté 3 cloves of finely chopped garlic and
1 large onion, finely chopped, in 3 T salad
oil. Add 1 lb ($\frac{1}{2}$ kg) finely minced beef. Fry
for 10 minutes. Add 1 tin of tomatoes
(16 oz or $\frac{1}{2}$ kg), 1 small tin tomato paste
(5 oz or 125 g), 1 t dried oregano, 1 t
sweet basil, 1 bay leaf and salt and pepper to

72

sweet basil
bay leaf
salt
pepper

taste. Simmer over low heat for 2 hours.

Assemble pizza

salami
Cheddar cheese
champignons
(optional)
stuffed olives
(optional)
green pepper
spring onions
meat sauce
pizza dough
Parmesan cheese
Serves: 12

Slice ¼ lb (100 g) salami and section into quarters. Grate ½ lb (¼ kg) Cheddar cheese. Slice contents of ½ small tin champignon mushrooms and slice ½ c stuffed olives (optional). Chop ½ c green pepper and finely slice ½ c spring onions.

Divide meat mixture between 4 prepared 10 inch pizza trays, making sure to spread evenly. Top with grated Cheddar cheese, followed by salami attractively arranged. Add chopped green pepper, spring onions, champignons, and sliced stuffed olives if desired. Sprinkle liberally with Parmesan cheese.

Bake in fairly hot oven (400° F) for 20 to 30 minutes or until dough is crisp and the top is brown and bubbly.

Note: Left over cold meat, smoked fish, bacon, or fresh mushrooms may all be used to vary the combinations of pizza.

Biscuit trays may be substituted quite satisfactorily for pizza trays. This freezes very well. Heat for 10 minutes in a moderate oven before serving.

Variations: Fish Pizza

Substitute fish for meat in tomato sauce. Fold 1 c cooked flaked fish into the sauce after it has been simmered for 2 hours. Serve topped with cheese, olives and spring onions.

Roti Pizza

Instead of preparing the dough for the base, large Roti, cooked and cooled, may be used (see p. 148). In this case 10 to 12 minutes in a hot oven will be sufficient.

73

Fish and other Sea and River Foods

In the Pacific Islands a wide variety of fish is used. These vary in size from the small river cigani or whitebait of Fiji, or sardine-like daniva which swims in shoals round many of the island groups, to walu and tuna weighing over a hundred pounds.

Many of the tropical varieties are equal to temperate climate fish in texture and flavour. It is well worth while finding out the most satisfactory varieties available from the local people.

When buying fish always ensure that the eyes are bright and full and the flesh is firm. Fish deteriorates very quickly in the tropics. In many places, certain fish are poisonous during the summer season. It is important to seek local advice.

In the Pacific Islands fish is traditionally cooked by simmering in water or coconut cream. Or it is wrapped in leaves, seasoned with coconut cream, salt and onions and then baked in an earth oven. Small fish are often grilled over the coals of a fire. Fish are preserved by salting, smoking and frying.

Raw fish, marinated in lemon juice (kokoda) is a popular dish throughout the area.

Fish are often sold whole in tropical markets and scales or skin must be removed at home. To scale a fish, scrape with a knife or scaler from tail to head—against "the grain". To skin a fish first remove head and fins. Insert the top of a sharp knife under the skin at the head end and round the sides. With a piece of cloth pull the skin head to tail.

Crabs, crayfish and prawns abound in tropical waters. There are many varieties, the majority of which have a good flavour and texture. Crustacea deteriorate rapidly in hot climates. When markets have no refrigeration people like to buy these sea and river foods alive. Tropical crustacea are usually cooked by simmering in water, the flesh is then removed from the body and claws and seasoned in many ways. The seasoned flesh is often served in the bright red crab and crayfish shells.

Fish Chart

Name	Appearance	Best Size to Choose	Preparation	Characteristics and How to Cook
BARRACUDA OGO	Dark grey upperside, grey belly, spiked mouth scales.	12–36 inches	Scale, remove fins and head. Fillet or cut in section.	Good flavour, white, fine texture, little fat. Best filleted and fried.
CORAL TROUT (Cod type) DONU	Similar to trout. Distinctive teeth. Colour varies red to brown. Spots vary in colour. Blue to brown scales.	Any size	Skin, remove fins, head, fillet fish. *Warning*: Eat only brown fish with blue spots. The red varieties are poisonous in some areas.	Very fine white flesh. Good flavour. Medium fat. Best filleted and fried.
HUMPED HEADED PARROT FISH KALIA	Like a bluish parrot fish with large lump on head—big scales.	5–7 lb in weight	Skin or scale, remove head and fins. Cut in fillets.	Excellent flavour and texture. Medium fat. White flesh. Any method of cooking.
MULLET KANACE	Grey with silver belly scales.	12–24 inches	Scale, remove head, fins. Fillet—taking care to avoid bones.	This fish has white flesh and a fine flavour and good texture, but is bony, fairly fat. Use for fish soup, fry or bake. Good for kokoda.
PARROT FISH ULAVI	Turquoise blue, green or red scales.	12–18 inches	Scale, remove fins and head. Fillet or cut in ½ inch cross sections.	This fish has a white very soft flesh. It must be used soon after catching. Flesh has fine flavour and texture. A fatty fish. Best fried. Do not overcook as flesh becomes soft.

75

Name	Appearance	Best Size to Choose	Preparation	Characteristics and How to Cook
RABBIT FISH NUQA	Smooth black grey skin. Spiny fins. Lighter grey belly.	8–14 inches long	Skin, remove head, fins, use whole, fillet or cut in ½ inch cross-sections.	This fish has a delicate flavour and fine flesh. Medium fat. Fry, grill, steam or bake.
SNAPPER TYPE KABATIA KAWAGO SAMBUTU	All these fish are very similar in appearance: Scales Kabatia—Greenish with black spot near eye. Kawago—Red grey yellow Distinctive head markings. Sambutu—Similar to Kawago but rounder shape.	12–18 inches	Remove scales and fins. Cut in ½ inch thick cross-sections or fillet. Leave whole for baking.	These fish have a good flavour and firm white flaky flesh, and are fairly lean. Fry, steam, roll in flour, sauté till brown and bake in casserole with tomatoes, onion and coconut cream or fresh milk. Bake whole—leave head on. Decorate with tomato and onion rings, season with salt, pepper, dot with butter. Cover with foil and cook at 350° F till tender. *Variation*: Stuff with seasoned bread stuffing.
JACK FISH TREVALLY SAQA	Grey, silver, smooth skin. Some varieties are black.	14–24 inches	Scale or skin, remove fins and head. Cut in fillets or ½ inch cross-sections or use whole.	The flesh is white and has a fine texture, of low fat content. It is inclined to be dry and is best cooked in a casserole with coconut cream or milk. May be baked whole as for Kabatia. Fried in fillets and served with a sauce. Excellent for sweet and sour fish.

SPANISH MACKEREL WALU	Silvery belly, dark grey blue upper side. Wavy fins on body. Smooth skin.	Any size	Scale or skin, remove fins and head. Cut in fillets or ½ inch cross sections. Cut in 2–3 lb sections for baking.	This fish has an excellent flavour, the flesh is fairly firm, white and flakes well when cooked. It is fairly lean. Steaks may be grilled, fillets fried, excellent cooked in casserole as for Kabatia. Make good kokoda (p. 36). Bake 2–3 lb sections and serve cold with mayonnaise or tartare sauce.
STINGRAY VAI	Flat with long tail— smooth skin—no bones.	14–24 inches	Skin, cut off wings. cut in fillets or steaks	The flesh has a good flavour. It is medium fat. White colour. Fillets may be fried, baked or steamed. Good for "made up" pies etc.
TUNA YELLOW FIN SKIP JACK BONITO DOGTOOTH YATU AKU	See illustrations.	4–15 lbs	Skin, remove head and fins. Use in fillets or cross sections. Remove dark soft flesh along backbone; this has a stronger flavour.	Yellow Fin—light red flesh, fine flavour. Skip Jack— darker flesh, stronger flavour. Bonito—darker flesh, stronger flavour. Dogtooth— finer white flesh—excellent flavour.

Uses: The Yellow Fin and Skip Jack make excellent sashimi (p. 84). Use Dogtooth for kokoda (p. 36). All types of tuna are best cooked in a casserole, or covered in foil and baked. Excellent served as cold fish steak (p. 82). Make good curries. Smoke and use as an appetiser. Make smoked Tuna pâté (p. 34).

Name	Appearance	Best Size to Choose	Preparation	Characteristics and How to Cook
CRAB Samoan, Mangrove QARI	Greenish grey shell. Large claws.	Large heavy crabs weighing ¾–1 lb (½ kg) or more. Should be alive when purchased in market.	Wash well.	Drop into boiling salted water, cover, return to the boil and simmer for 15 minutes or until bright red. Joints of claws should then be loose. When cold cut through centre of under shell. Break claws and remove flesh. Season flesh with sauce, miti, or mayonnaise. Serve in salads, in shell, creamed or baked. Make Qari vali (p. 85). A delicious seafood.
CRAWFISH— MANGROVE MANA	Reddish brown.	Larger mana weighing 6–8 oz (200 g). Should be alive when purchased in market	Wash to remove mud.	Cook as for crabs. Use in similar ways. Has a distinctive sweet flavour.
CRAYFISH URAU	Pinkish green body, darker feelers.	Any size—1–2 lbs (½–1 kg). Contain fair amount of flesh. Should be alive or freshly caught when purchased.	Wash.	Place in hot water. Bring to simmering point. Cook till bright red and joints become loose. Cut through centre under shell and remove flesh. Crack claws. Save back shell. Use in salads, in cheese sauce or with mayonnaise. In any lobster recipe. Excellent flavour.

FRESH WATER MUSSELS KAI	Black shells.	Larger shells.	Soak in water 1–2 days to remove sand	Place in a pot of water and bring to boil. Simmer till shells open. Remove fish. Cut off tough "beards". Use in soups (p. 47). May also be curried or served in sauce, though rather tough.
RIVER PRAWNS URA	Greenish grey.	4–5 inches long	Wash.	Place in hot water and bring to simmering point. Cooked when bright red. Remove from shell.
SEA PRAWNS KING & TIGER PRAWNS	Greenish grey.	4–8 inches long	Wash.	Cook as above. Use all kinds cold in salads, serve with miti, in cheese sauce, with mayonnaise. Use in curries and many prawn recipes. Make Prawns in Coconut Sauce (p. 84)

Name	Appearance	Best Size to Choose	Preparation	Characteristics and How to Cook
TURTLE VONU DINA TAKU	Green Turtle (vonu dina) smooth shell. Taku—Hawkbill—head has sharp bill. Back is scaly.	Larger size have better flavour. Taku has a stronger fishy flavour.	Lay on back—cut round breastplate. Remove this. Leg joints are then cut out. Remove flesh from joints. Every part of the turtle may be used.	Turtle meat is like veal in texture. The best meat comes from the forepart of the turtle. The green fat has a fine flavour and some of this should be included with the meat in all recipes. Cut flesh into steaks, making sure that meat is cut across the grain. Keep the green fat. Use the whiter flesh in veal type recipes. Cut in cubes and bake in casseroles (p. 87).

Kalia puff

kalia or
white fish fillets
flour
salt
margarine
water
butter
parsley
pepper, salt
egg yolk
Serves: 6

Cut 1 lb ($\frac{1}{2}$ kg) fresh or thawed kalia or any white fish into thin fillets. Prepare flaky pastry as follows. Prepare plain Short Crust Pastry using 2 c flour, 1 t salt, $\frac{1}{2}$ c margarine and water. Roll out pastry to half inch thickness. Place $\frac{1}{2}$ c margarine on the top half of the pastry in the centre. Fold up bottom, and turn in sides. Repeat rolling and refolding 3 more times. If it becomes too sticky while rolling, place in refrigerator to chill for a few minutes. Chill for at least one hour before using. Roll out chilled pastry until it is about 9 inches wide, 12 inches long and $\frac{1}{4}$ inch thick. Place fish fillets down the centre, leaving about 1 inch at each end. Evenly dot top with $\frac{1}{4}$ c butter mixed with 1 T finely chopped parsley. Season with a little salt and pepper. Fold ends up over fish and then sides to meet in the middle. If desired, decorate with fancy pastry shapes. Brush with beaten egg yolk or milk. Bake in hot oven (425° F) for 15 minutes, then reduce heat to moderate (350° F) and continue baking for another 15 to 20 minutes. It should be crisp and a delicate brown when cooked.
Cut into wedges and serve.
A perfect lunch or supper dish which may be prepared well ahead of time and just popped from refrigerator to oven half an hour before serving.

Fish curry

ghee or oil
onion
garlic
curry powder
tomatoes or
    tomato paste

Place 2 T oil or ghee in a saucepan and heat. Add 1 medium onion finely chopped and 1 crushed clove of garlic and fry lightly. Add 1 T curry powder. Stir well, reduce heat, and cook for a few minutes. Add 1 T tomato paste or $\frac{1}{2}$ lb ($\frac{1}{4}$ kg) chopped tomatoes.

F

81

water	Stir well. Add sufficient water to make
salt	a thick sauce. Season to taste with salt and
lemon juice	2 t lemon juice. Place $1\frac{1}{2}$ lb ($\frac{3}{4}$ kg) fish fillets
fish fillets	in the sauce and simmer gently till soft.
Serves: 6	Refer to notes on curry powders (p. 18).

Prawn, fish and rice scallop

garlic	Sauté $\frac{1}{2}$ crushed clove garlic and 1 T finely
onion	chopped onion in 3 T melted butter. Stir in
butter	3 T flour. Gradually add $\frac{1}{2}$ c fish stock and
flour	$\frac{1}{2}$ c tomato purée. Season with salt and
fish stock	pepper. Bring to a boil and cook for 2 to 3
tomato purée	minutes. Stir in 1 c rich milk, 2 T dry
salt	sherry and $\frac{1}{2}$ c grated cheese. Add $\frac{1}{2}$ to $\frac{3}{4}$ c
pepper	cooked coarsely chopped prawns (save a
rich milk	few whole ones to garnish the dish), $1\frac{1}{2}$ c
dry sherry	cooked flaked fish such as walu or saga and
cheese	$1\frac{1}{2}$ c cooked rice to the sauce.
prawns	Place mixture in a greased baking dish.
fish	Slice remaining prawns in half. Decorate
rice	the top, alternating prawns and slices of
tomatoes	tomato. Sprinkle with $\frac{1}{4}$ c grated cheese.
Serves: 4–6	Bake in 350° F oven until brown and
	heated through. Do not overcook.
	Variation: Add 2 T finely chopped green
	pepper or 1 T finely chopped celery to the
	sauce.

Cold fish steak

walu, tuna	Use a 2–3 lb ($1-1\frac{1}{2}$ kg) piece of walu, tuna
or white fish	or any similar fish. Remove the skin and
lemon juice	place in a casserole. Add 2 T lemon juice,
salt	1 t salt, and some chopped fresh dill to $2\frac{1}{2}$ c
dill	water. Pour over the fish. Cover fish with 1
water	small sliced onion. Add a bay leaf and 3 or 4
onion	peppercorns. Cover casserole and bake in a
bay leaf	300° F oven for approximately 1 hour or
peppercorns	until fish is tender. Leave in stock until cold.
Serves: 8 to 10	Serve fish flaked or cut in thin slices across
	the grain, with salad and a good mayonnaise
	flavoured with chopped capers.

Fish in rou rou leaves

fish fillets
rou rou leaves
salt
onion
coconut cream
tomato
Serves: 6

Cut $1\frac{1}{2}$ lb ($\frac{3}{4}$ kg) fish fillet into servings approximately 2–3 inches long and $1\frac{1}{2}$ inches thick. Remove the stalks from 12 large rou rou leaves. Place 2 leaves together, making sure that the holes where the stalk was removed are covered and top side is up. Place the fish in the centre of the leaves. Sprinkle with a little salt, finely chopped onion and 1 T coconut cream. Fold up the fish in the leaves and secure with a toothpick. Place the "parcels" in a casserole. Pour 2 c coconut cream over the "parcels". Cover casserole with a lid and bake for 30 minutes at 350° F. To add colour to this dish, place a slice of tomato on top of each "parcel".

Fish in coconut sauce

fish fillets
coconut cream
onion
salt
chilli
cornflour
oil
tomato
seasoned flour
Serves: 6

Cut $1\frac{1}{2}$ lb ($\frac{3}{4}$ kg) fish into servings. Prepare 2 c coconut cream. Place in saucepan with 2 T finely chopped onion, 1 t salt, a little chopped chilli (may be omitted) and 1 T cornflour mixed to a paste with a little of the cold cream. Bring to boiling point, stirring all the time. Do not allow sauce to boil as it will become lumpy. Keep the sauce at simmering point for 2–3 minutes and then remove from heat. Dip pieces of fish in seasoned flour and brown in hot oil. Place in a casserole and pour sauce over. Garnish with slices of tomato. Bake at 300° F for 20 minutes.
Variation: Add 1 T lemon juice.

Egg fish pie

shortcrust pastry
eggs
cream
mackerel
salt

Prepare Short Crust Pastry. Line a 9 inch plate with pastry.
Prepare filling by beating 4 eggs well. Add $\frac{1}{4}$ c heavy cream to eggs, followed by an 8 oz ($\frac{1}{4}$ kg) tin flaked mackerel or cooked

83

lemon juice
parsley
tomato
Serves: 6

fish, 1 t salt, 2 t lemon juice and 1 T chopped parsley. Mix well. Pour into prepared pie shell, garnish with slices of tomato and with a further tablespoon of finely chopped parsley. Bake in a moderately hot oven, about 400° F, for 20 to 30 minutes. When done it will be firm, golden brown and slightly raised.

Fried spiced fish
fish fillets
milk
flour
salt
curry powder
oil
coconut cream
Serves: 6

Cut 1½–2 lb (¾–1 kg) filleted fish into servings and dip in milk. Mix two thirds c flour with 1 t salt and 1 t curry powder. Dip the pieces of fish in this mixture and fry till golden brown in hot oil. Cover fish with 1½ c coconut cream and bake for 15 minutes in a medium oven, 300–350° F. Serve with lemon slices or pickled limes.

Sashimi
filleted skip jack
or yellow fin tuna
ginger or mustard
Japanese soy sauce
Serves: as desired

Cut fillets across the grain into slices ¼ inch thick. Flavour soy sauce with mixed mustard or grated fresh ginger using 1 t to ½ c soy sauce, or to taste. Dip slices of fish in sauce and eat at once.
Variation: Use garlic, chilli or spring onion in sauce.

Shellfish

River or sea prawns should be alive if bought in the market. Wash well and put into boiling water with a little salt. Simmer about 5 minutes, depending on the size. Remove from heat and drain. When cool, remove the head and shell.
Prawns are delicious used in place of fish in Fish in Rou Rou Leaves and Fish in Coconut Sauce.

Prawns in coconut sauce

Prepare coconut sauce as directed for Fish in Coconut Sauce (p. 83). Add 3 c (¾ kg)

84

cooked, peeled chopped prawns and simmer until just warmed through.

Prawns in rou rou leaves

Prepare Fish in Rou Rou Leaves (p. 83), substituting 3 c ($\frac{3}{4}$ kg) cooked peeled prawns for fish fillets.

Tempura (butterfly) prawns

fresh prawns
salt
water

Boil 24 large fresh prawns in salted water. Cool, remove heads and shells from body, leaving tails intact. Make a deep slit along back (to butterfly) removing black vein as you do so. Flatten prawns.
Note : Frozen prawns may be used if the tail is still on.

Batter

flour
salt
baking powder
eggs
water
fat or oil

Sift $1\frac{1}{2}$ c flour, $\frac{1}{4}$ t salt and $\frac{1}{4}$ t baking powder together. Beat in 2 eggs and 1 to $1\frac{1}{2}$ c water. Dip prawns in batter, let excess run off and then fry in deep very hot fat or oil until golden and crisp. Put aside to drain and keep warm.

Sauce (Piquant)

beef stock
soy sauce
sugar
horseradish
monosodium
  glutamate
Serves: 4

Bring 1 c beef stock to a boil. Add $\frac{1}{4}$ c soy sauce, 2 t sugar, 2 t fresh horseradish or $\frac{1}{4}$ t dry horseradish and 1 t monosodium glutamate.

SERVE

Serve prawns over mound of rice. Garnish with pepper rings and a small dish of sauce on the side. Prawns are picked up by the tail with the fingers and dipped in sauce.

Qari vali (crab)

crab
salt

Cook 1 medium size crab in boiling salted water until done. Cool and remove the

85

water
onion
garlic
tomato
oil
pepper
eggs
Serves: 4

meat. Keep the body part of the shell. Fry 1 medium size chopped onion, 3 finely chopped cloves of garlic and 1 large tomato, peeled and chopped, in 2 T oil until golden. Add crab, ½ t salt and a dash of pepper. Stir fry for 5 minutes.

Add 2 beaten eggs and stir until just cooked. Place mixture in a clean crab shell and bake for 3 to 4 minutes at 400° F or serve as is.

Note: Tinned crab and small ramekins may be used if fresh crab is not available.

Qari vakasoso (crab)

crab
Chinese cabbage
water
salt
onion
tomato
coconut
very thick coconut
  cream
Serves: 4

Boil and remove the meat from 1 large crab (2 c or 250 g). Shred finely the leaves from 1 bunch of Chinese cabbage and boil in salted water. Strain and put aside.

Finely chop 1 medium size onion. Peel and chop 1 medium size tomato. Grate 1 coconut, leaving a good coating of coconut in the shell. Put the shell aside.

Mix crab, tomato, onion, cabbage and 2 T grated coconut together. Place in coconut shell and squeeze ¼ c very thick coconut cream over the top. Place the lid on the coconut and put in a saucepan with water to steam for 10 minutes. Serve in shell.

This may be prepared with crab as given, or with any available combination of seafood or fish. Excellent for a buffet dinner.

Note: Care must be taken to cut the coconut shell neatly in half.

Duruka crayfish

crayfish
duruka
salt
water
onion
green pepper

Have on hand 1 lb (½ kg) cooked crayfish. Drop 12 medium size duruka into 2 c boiling salted water and simmer for 15 minutes. Strain and save the liquid. Finely chop ½ c onion and ¼ c green pepper. Fry until transparent in 4 T butter.

butter
milk or coconut
  cream
lemon juice
flour
salt
pepper
Serves: 6

Chop and add crayfish to onion mixture and stir fry for 5 minutes.
Add 1 c milk or coconut cream, and 2 t lemon juice to ½ c flour.
Add duruka water to milk mixture and simmer until thick. Add onion, crayfish and duruka. Season to taste with salt and pepper. Serve over rice or noodles as a main course.

Turtle casserole

turtle meat
salt
pepper
lemon rind
chilli
seasoned flour
onion
oil
water or coconut
  cream
Serves: 6

Cut 1½ lb (¾ kg) turtle meat into ½ inch cubes, making sure that a little of the green fat is included. Season with salt, pepper, grated rind of 1 lemon and chopped chilli. Let the meat stand for 1 to 2 hours. Shake the meat in a paper bag with 1 c seasoned flour until it is well covered. Sauté 1 medium sized chopped onion in ½ c oil in a saucepan, add turtle and sauté until brown. Place in a casserole, pour over 2 c water or coconut cream, cover with foil or a lid and bake at 300° F for 1½ hours.

Steamed turtle kovu

turtle meat
banana leaves
salt
pepper
onion
chilli
water
Serves: 6

Cube 1½ lb (¾ kg) turtle meat including some of the green fat. Hold 2 small banana leaves over a flame until they become soft and pliable.
Season turtle meat with 1 t salt, pepper, 1 finely chopped onion and a little chilli. Place mixture on a banana leaf, and tie up firmly. Cover with a second leaf, and place the bundle (kovu) on a stand in a saucepan half filled with water. Steam for 2 hours.
Variation: Lemon juice or tomato may be added to the meat for extra flavour.

NAMES OF FISH COMMONLY CAUGHT IN TROPICAL WATERS

Common Name	Scientific Name
Barracuda	Sphyraenella spp.
Coral trout	Plectropoma spp.
Jack Fish—Trevally	Caranx spp.
Mullet	Mugil cephalus
Parrot fish	Callyodon spp.
Rabbit fish	Siganus spp.
Rock Cod	Epinephelus spp.
Snapper (1)	Lethrinus nebulosus
Snapper (2)	Lethrinus spp.
Skipjack	Katsuvonus pelamis
Spanish mackerel	Scomberomorus commersoni
Stingray	Amphoristius
Yellow Fin	Neothunnus macropterus

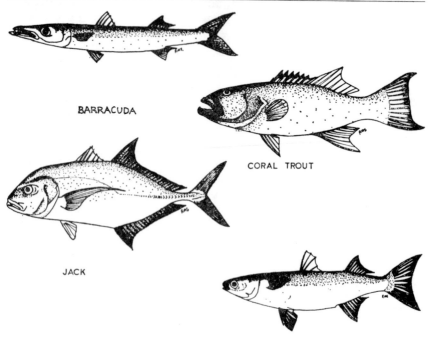

BARRACUDA

CORAL TROUT

JACK

MULLET

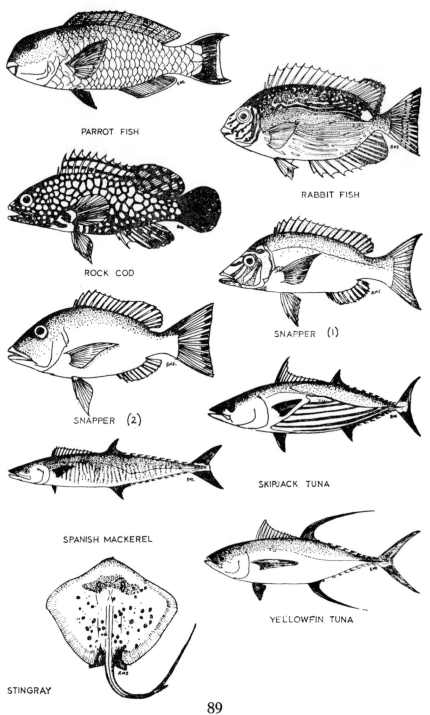

PARROT FISH

RABBIT FISH

ROCK COD

SNAPPER (1)

SNAPPER (2)

SKIPJACK TUNA

SPANISH MACKEREL

YELLOWFIN TUNA

STINGRAY

Lamb and Mutton

All meat should be kept for at least 4 days after killing before it is used. During this time the meat matures and becomes tender. The maturing process takes place at cool, but not freezing temperatures. Mutton or lamb is often frozen in a fresh state, so it is important to keep frozen meat for 2–3 days before cooking. Keep at the bottom of the refrigerator. Make certain that the joint is kept dry and remove any liquid that forms after defrosting. The quality of lamb or mutton varies. Always inquire whether it is first or second grade. In general, second grade meat contains more fat, and in the case of mutton, the sheep is older. Second grade meat needs more careful cooking. To ensure that mutton is tender, do the following:

(a) Cook for a longer time at a lower temperature.
(b) Marinate overnight in a flavoured acid marinade, see p. 98.
(c) Marinate in a soy sauce mixture, see p. 98.

The following flavourings add richness and variety to lamb and mutton: rosemary, mint, thyme, sage, ginger, mace, fennel, garlic, turmeric, cardamom, lemon, soy sauce, tomato. (See also p. 16.)

Cinnamon mango short loin chops

short loin lamb chops
salt
pepper
mango
cinnamon
Serves: as desired

Grill short loin lamb chops seasoned with salt and pepper in the usual way. Just before they are done, remove from the grill, place thin slices of raw mango on each chop and sprinkle liberally with powdered cinnamon. Return to grill and cook until mango is soft and slightly brown. Remove carefully and serve.

Pineapple forequarter chops

forequarter lamb
chops
salt
pepper
pineapple
maraschino cherries
Serves: as desired

Grill forequarter lamb chops seasoned with salt and pepper in the usual way. Just before they are done, remove from grill and top each chop with a slice of fresh or tinned pineapple and half a maraschino cherry. Return to grill and cook until pineapple is beginning to brown (3 to 5 minutes). Serve immediately.

Coconut mint short loin chops

coconut
flour
mint
egg
water
short loin
  lamb chops
salt
pepper
mint sauce
Serves: 4

Mix 1 c freshly grated coconut, ½ c flour and 2 T finely chopped fresh mint together. Beat 1 egg with 1 T water. Season 8 short loin lamb chops with salt and pepper. Dip in egg and then in coconut mixture, coating both sides evenly. Press down firmly with fingers. Refrigerate for at least 2 hours.
Grill in the usual way, being particularly careful not to disturb the coconut batter during turning. Alternatively, cook in baking pan at 375° F, 10 to 15 minutes or until crisp.
Serve with fresh mint sauce.

Marinated lamb chops

lamb chops
oil
garlic
parsley
basil
salt
black pepper
prepared French
  mustard
anchovy sauce
lemon juice
Serves: 4 to 6

Trim excess fat off 2 lb (1 kg) forequarter lamb chops. Mix ¼ c oil, ½ clove crushed garlic, 1 T finely chopped parsley, and 1 t chopped fresh basil, 1 t salt and freshly ground black pepper together. Cover chops with marinade and leave for 4–5 hours.
Mix 2 T prepared French mustard, 1 T anchovy sauce, juice of ½ lemon, ½ crushed clove garlic and freshly ground pepper together. Spread some of the mixture on one side of chops and then grill. When brown turn over, spread with remaining mixture and grill other side. Alternatively, cook in baking pan for 10 to 15 minutes at 375° F.

Baked leg of lamb eastern style

leg of lamb
onion
garlic
green ginger
oil
sesame oil
soy sauce or salt

Trim excess fat from a 5 lb (2½ kg) leg of lamb and place in a baking dish. Score the skin with a sharp knife. Mince or purée in blender 1 medium onion, 1 clove garlic and ½ inch piece green ginger together. Add ¼ c oil, 1 T sesame oil, 1 T soy sauce or 1 t salt, and ½ t freshly ground black pepper.

91

black pepper
water or stock
cornflour
Serves: 6 to 8

Pour mixture over lamb. Place in a 325° F oven and bake for 2½ hours. Baste periodically during cooking. Remove excess fat from pan drippings. Add some water or stock and thicken with cornflour in the proportion of 2 t cornflour to 1 c liquid.
Note : For a more delicate flavour omit soy sauce, and use 1 t salt.

Baked lamb with eggplant sauce

leg of lamb
oil
red wine or vinegar
peppercorns
salt
garlic
onion
eggplant
stock or water
Serves: 6 to 8

Trim the excess fat from a 4–5 lb (2–3 kg) leg of lamb. Score skin and place in a baking dish. Put ½ c oil, ¼ c red wine or vinegar, 1 t peppercorns, 1 t salt, 1 clove garlic and 1 small onion in a blender. Pour the blended mixture over the leg of lamb and leave to marinate for 2 to 3 hours. Cover and place in 300° F oven. Bake for 2 hours. Remove cover and bake at 350° F for ½ to 1 hour.

Bake 2 whole unpeeled eggplant (total weight ½ lb) for 1 hour. When done, cut in half, scoop out flesh and purée.

Remove lamb to a platter to keep warm. Remove excess drippings from pan. Mix eggplant purée with remaining dripping. Add sufficient stock or water to make a thick sauce. Check seasoning. Simmer for 5 to 10 minutes.

Variation : Mix 2 T flour with drippings. Add 1 c stock, ½ c red wine and stir until thick. Simmer for 5 minutes. Strain. Add 2 T cream just before serving.

Baked lamb with crumb crust

leg of lamb
egg
butter
breadcrumbs
onion
garlic
thyme, fresh

Take 4–5 lb (2–3 kg) leg of lamb and remove as much fat as possible with a sharp knife. Leave just a thin layer. Brush with 1 beaten egg.

Soften ½ c butter and gradually add 1½ c dried breadcrumbs, ½ small minced onion, ½ clove crushed garlic, 1 t fresh thyme, ½:

92

sage, fresh
black pepper
salt
Serves: 6 to 8

fresh sage (well chopped), $\frac{1}{2}$ t black pepper and 1 t salt. Knead mixture well and spread over the lamb evenly. Bake in 325° F oven for 2 to 2$\frac{1}{2}$ hours. Turn the dish around several times while baking to ensure even browning. The lamb will have a golden crust when cooked. Remove carefully and place on serving dish. Excellent cold.

Note: A few teaspoons of boiling water may be added to crumb mixture if necessary to make it more pliable.

Coconut lamb shoulder casserole

onions
oil
boned lamb
  shoulder
white wine
tomato soup
water
cornflour
sour cream
salt
black pepper
marjoram, dried
Serves: 6

Peel, cube and fry 2 c onions until golden in $\frac{1}{4}$ c oil in a large saucepan. Add about 2 lb (1 kg) boned chopped shoulder of lamb. Add $\frac{1}{2}$ c each white wine, tinned tomato soup and water.

Simmer for 1$\frac{1}{2}$ to 2 hours or until meat is tender. Thicken with 2 T cornflour gradually mixed with $\frac{1}{4}$ c water. Season with 2 t salt, $\frac{1}{4}$ t freshly ground black pepper and $\frac{1}{2}$ t dried marjoram. Stir in 1 c sour cream just before serving.

Serve over buttered egg noodles with fresh grated coconut sprinkled on top.

Madras mutton curry

lean mutton
ghee, butter or oil
garlic
onions
curry powder
tomato paste or
  fresh tomatoes
salt
lemon juice
Serves: 6

Cut 1$\frac{1}{2}$ lb ($\frac{3}{4}$ kg) mutton (leg or shoulder) into cubes. Heat 2 oz (50 g) ghee, butter or oil in a saucepan and add 1 crushed clove garlic and 1 finely chopped large onion. Cook until onion starts to colour. Add 1 T good curry powder. Stir well and fry for a few minutes. Add meat, 1 T tomato paste or 2–3 chopped tomatoes, 1–2 t salt and 1 T lemon juice. Stir well and then cook slowly until meat is tender. A little stock or water may be added to make more sauce if desired.

Note: Curry powder, p. 18.

93

Kofta curry

garlic
onion
minced lamb or beef
pepper
cinnamon
ground cloves
egg
butter, ghee or
  cooking oil
turmeric
coriander
ginger
chilli powder
coconut cream
salt
lemon juice
Serves: 6

Mince 1 clove garlic and 1 small onion. Combine with 1 lb ($\frac{1}{2}$ kg) finely minced lamb or beef. Add $\frac{1}{4}$ t each pepper, powdered cinnamon and ground cloves and 1 beaten egg. Form into balls with floured hands. Fry in $\frac{1}{2}$ c butter, ghee or oil until golden brown. Remove.
Fry 1 large finely sliced onion in remaining fat until golden. Add 1 t each ground turmeric, coriander, $\frac{1}{2}$ t ginger and a little chilli powder. Sauté spices 3–4 minutes. Pour 2 c coconut cream over spices and onion. Add 1 t salt and 1 t lemon juice. Add meat balls and simmer gently for $\frac{1}{2}$ hour. Cook 1$\frac{1}{2}$ c rice and serve with curry.
Note : If mince is coarse put through mincer twice.

Mutton or lamb korma

mutton or lamb
  cutlets
garlic
green ginger
yoghurt
onion
cloves
cardamom pods
cinnamon stick
butter or ghee
salt
coconut cream
Serves: 6

Trim the fat off about 2 lb (1 kg) lamb or mutton cutlets. Crush 1 clove garlic and 1 t green ginger to a pulp. Mix with $\frac{1}{2}$ c yoghurt. Brush over chops and leave for several hours.
Finely slice 1 large onion. Bruise 6 cloves, 4 cardamom pods and a 2 inch stick of cinnamon with a rolling pin. Heat 2 oz butter, ghee or oil in saucepan. Sauté onions and then spices. Cook for 4–5 minutes or until onions are soft but not brown. Add the meat, and an additional $\frac{1}{2}$ c yoghurt and 1–2 t salt. Cover with lid and simmer until meat is cooked. If desired add 1 c coconut cream or additional yoghurt may be added if desired. Cook 1$\frac{1}{2}$ c rice and serve with Korma.

Lamb and eggplant escalope

lamb
onion
garlic
eggplant
butter
flour
stock
rich milk
bay leaf
rosemary, dried
breadcrumbs
Serves: 6

A way of using cooked lamb:
Cut 12 oz (300 g) cooked lamb in small cubes. Slice 1 medium size onion and finely chop 1 clove garlic. Peel and slice 2 eggplant or sufficient to yield 6 ounces (150 g). Sauté onion and garlic in ¼ c butter. Add eggplant and sauté until golden brown. Add extra butter if necessary. Remove eggplant, onion and garlic, leaving pan juices. Prepare a sauce with pan juices, 3 T flour, 1½ c stock and 1 c rich milk. Season with 1 bay leaf and ½ t dried rosemary. Simmer for 5 minutes. Place alternate layers of lamb, onion and eggplant in a casserole and pour over sauce. Sprinkle with ½ c soft breadcrumbs mixed with 1 T melted butter. Bake in 350° F oven for 30 minutes or until brown.
Variation: Combine all ingredients in a saucepan, heat and serve with plain or pilau rice.

Veal

Good veal should have a pale pink colour and fine texture. Like other meats, it must be properly matured to make it tender. Darker coloured veal comes from more mature animals. To make this tender, pound well and use the marinades as given on page 98 under beef.
Veal has a delicate flavour which can be enhanced by the addition of lemon, white wine, parsley, sage, thyme, oregano, onion, garlic, tomato, sour cream, yoghurt and cheese.
Veal is best served with rich, delicately flavoured sauces and stuffings.

Veal with tuna sauce

leg veal or steak
lemon juice

Tie 2½–3 lb (2–2½ kg) whole piece veal together with a string and place in a

water
anchovy sauce
salt
pepper
bay leaves
onion
cloves
tuna
capers
lemon juice
black pepper
mayonnaise
Serves: 6–8

casserole. Combine $\frac{1}{2}$ c lemon juice, 2 c water, $1\frac{1}{2}$ T anchovy sauce, 1 t salt and $\frac{1}{2}$ t pepper. Pour over meat. Add 2 bay leaves, $\frac{1}{2}$ sliced onion and 4 cloves. Cover and bake 2–$2\frac{1}{2}$ hours at 300° F. Leave in stock until cold.
Prepare sauce by finely mashing 6 oz (150 g) tuna with a fork and combining with $1\frac{1}{2}$ T anchovy sauce, 1 T chopped capers, 2 T lemon juice, $\frac{1}{2}$ t freshly ground black pepper $\frac{1}{2}$ t salt and $\frac{1}{2}$ c mayonnaise. Take veal out of stock. Remove string and pour over sauce. Refrigerate overnight.
Serve cold on platter, garnished with chopped parsley and accompanied by a salad.

Mushroom veal

veal steak
flour
salt
pepper
butter
oil
garlic
chicken stock
cornflour
dry white wine
tomato paste
onion
tomato
champignons
  (button
  mushrooms)
parsley
Serves: 6 to 8

Cut 2 lb (1 kg) veal steak or fillet into $1\frac{1}{2}$ inch squares about $\frac{1}{2}$ inch thick. Combine $\frac{1}{2}$ c flour with 1 t salt and $\frac{1}{4}$ t pepper. Dredge veal in seasoned flour and then fry in hot pan in a mixture of 2 T butter and 2 T oil. When brown, remove and keep warm.
Mince 3 medium cloves garlic and fry until golden, adding a little more oil if necessary. Slowly add 2 c chicken stock to which 2 T cornflour has been added. Stir to form a smooth gravy. Add $\frac{1}{2}$ c dry white wine and 2 T tomato paste. Simmer for 1 minute. Check seasoning. Place veal in a casserole dish and pour gravy over the top. Peel and quarter 4 medium size onions. Place on top of veal in casserole and cover with lid. Bake in 325° F oven for 1 hour.
Peel and cut 3 medium size tomatoes into 8ths. Place them on top of the veal along with 1 c drained champignons. Bake covered for a further 20 minutes. Gently stir mushrooms, tomatoes and onion into veal

just before serving. Lastly stir $\frac{1}{4}$ c finely chopped parsley into veal. (Don't do this too early or the parsley will become overcooked and lose its nice green colour.) Serve with rice or noodles.

Rou rou veal

veal steak
rou rou
Cheddar cheese
seasoned flour
egg
water
cornflake or
    breadcrumbs
butter
oil
Yield: as desired

Prepare veal steak by pounding until thin. Place 2 T cooked chopped rou rou on each slice of veal, followed by thin slices of Cheddar cheese. Fold in half and secure with a toothpick. Dip veal in seasoned flour and then in beaten egg to which 1 T water has been added. Press cornflake or bread crumbs onto veal.
Refrigerate for 1 to 2 hours.
Fry in moderately hot pan with $\frac{1}{2}$ butter, $\frac{1}{2}$ oil, cooking 5 to 7 minutes on each side. Serve immediately.

Kora veal birds

veal
onion
breadcrumbs
egg
rosemary
salt
black pepper
garlic
seasoned flour
butter
chicken stock
reduced cream
kora
lemon
Serves: 6

Have on hand $1\frac{1}{2}$ lb ($\frac{3}{4}$ kg) veal steak, about $\frac{1}{4}$ inch thick. Mince 6 oz (150 g) veal with 1 small onion. Stir in $\frac{1}{2}$ c breadcrumbs, 1 beaten egg, $\frac{1}{4}$ t rosemary, $\frac{1}{2}$ t salt and $\frac{1}{4}$ t freshly ground black pepper.
Pound remaining veal and cut into pieces 2 × 4 inches. Rub with a clove of garlic. Place 1 T stuffing on each piece veal. Roll and fasten with toothpick.
Dredge with seasoned flour and brown in hot butter in frypan. Add 1 c chicken stock, cover and simmer for 1 hour.
Remove veal to serving plate and keep hot. Stir $\frac{1}{2}$ c reduced cream (very thick tinned cream) and 1 T Kora into pan juices. Add a little water if too much of the pan juices have evaporated.
Serve sauce over veal with a slice of lemon.

G

97

Beef

The quality of beef can be highly variable in tropical climates. In some places the choicest plantation reared beef is available, whilst in others, the housewife must be content with miscellaneous pieces of meat from animals of unknown age.

Beef is tough for the following reasons:

The animal may be old and in poor condition when slaughtered. The carcass may be poorly butchered. When this happens tougher parts of the beast are often included with the more tender cuts.

Good quality beef is sometimes sold before it has matured. Beef must hang for 3 to 4 days at about 50° F to enable the tenderizing process to take place. Freshly killed beef should be kept in the bottom of the refrigerator, loosely covered for 3 to 4 days before using. Remove any liquor that forms and turn over daily.

With these thoughts in mind, we suggest the following ideas for making beef tender.

For steak or stewing meat of unknown origin, marinate for 4–5 hours in one of these mixtures:

1. $\frac{1}{4}$ c lemon juice, $\frac{1}{4}$ c salad oil, $\frac{1}{2}$ t salt, $\frac{1}{2}$ t pepper, $\frac{1}{2}$ crushed clove garlic or replace lemon juice with wine.
2. $\frac{1}{8}$ c soy sauce, $\frac{1}{4}$ c salad oil, 2 t chopped onion, 1 t crushed green ginger.
3. Cook tough steak at a low temperature, 250°–300° F, with plenty of tomato, or other acid fruit or use chopped green or ripe pawpaw and pineapple.

The above preparations are sufficient for $1\frac{1}{2}$ lb ($\frac{3}{4}$ kg) meat.

Steak with green pepper

tender steak
fillet or rump
cornflour
onion
green peppers
tomatoes
oil
beef stock
soy sauce
Serves: 6

Cut 1 lb ($\frac{1}{2}$ kg) tender steak into very thin slices, across the grain. Dip slices in $\frac{1}{2}$ c cornflour. Cut 1 medium sized onion, 2 large green peppers and 2 or 3 tomatoes into thin slices. Heat 3 T oil in a frying pan. Sauté sliced onions until golden. Add steak and sauté until brown. Add sliced peppers and stir fry 7–10 minutes. Stir in 2 c stock, 2 T soy sauce and lastly sliced tomatoes. Cook for another 5 minutes. Serve with rice.

Variation: Add 1 t crushed green ginger. Replace tomatoes with 1 c diced fresh pineapple.

Steak baigan (eggplant)

fillet steak
oil
prepared French mustard
eggplant
milk
seasoned flour
Serves: as desired

Cut fillets in pieces 1 inch thick. Spread with a little prepared French mustard and pan fry in a little hot oil. Cut slices of eggplant ½ inch thick. Dip in milk and then in seasoned flour. Fry till crisp and drain off oil on brown paper. Serve steak on slices of eggplant. Garnish with parsley butter (see p. 32).

Steak and pineapple

fillet steak
salt, black pepper
pineapple
oil
Serves: as desired

Season steak with salt and black pepper. Pan fry in oil or grill marinated fillet steak (soy or lemon juice marinade). Serve with slices of fried pineapple.

Beef in beer

A good recipe for tough beef.

beef steak
seasoned flour
butter
oil
onion
sugar
garlic
thyme
tomato paste
salt
beer
bay leaf
bread
prepared French mustard
Serves: 6

Cut 2 lb (1 kg) beef steak, suitable for braising, into ½ inch × 2 inch pieces. Dip in seasoned flour and brown in mixture of 2 T hot butter and 1 T hot oil. Remove from pan and place in casserole. Sauté 2 large sliced onions in pan. Sprinkle with 2 t sugar. This gives a good brown colour. Add onions to beef. Mix ½ crushed garlic clove, ½ t finely chopped thyme, 2 t tomato paste and 1 t salt with 1 c beer. Pour sauce over the meat. Add additional beer if necessary to cover. Place a bay leaf on top. Spread a thick slice of bread (½ inch thick) with prepared French mustard and place on top of meat. Cover casserole and cook for 2 hours at 250°–300° F. When done the beer should have evaporated.

99

Boiled corned beef

A well-cooked piece of corned beef (i.e. salt beef) provides an excellent main course for lunches, suppers and buffet meals.

corned silverside
or brisket
water
peppercorns
vinegar
sugar
cloves
bay leaf
Serves: as desired

Select a piece of silverside or brisket without too much fat. Weigh and allow 35 to 40 minutes cooking time per lb ($\frac{1}{2}$ kg). Place in a large saucepan and cover with water. Season with 4 to 5 peppercorns, $\frac{1}{2}$ c vinegar, $\frac{1}{2}$ to 1 c sugar, 3-4 cloves and 1 bay leaf. Bring to boiling point, reduce heat and simmer for remaining time. Cool in cooking water.

Note: If meat is very salt, soak for several hours in cold water before cooking. Cook in a large pot with ample water.

Orange glazed corned beef

boiled corned beef
marmalade
Serves: as desired

Prepare Boiled Corned Beef. Remove from saucepan, 20 minutes before end of cooking-time, spread thickly with about $\frac{1}{2}$ c marmalade and bake for about 20 minutes at 350° F.

Variation:

Pineapple glazed corned beef

Use drained, crushed pineapple and sugar in place of marmalade. Bake as directed.

Palusami casserole

rou rou leaves
onions
tinned corned beef
coconut cream
salt
chilli
Serves: 6

Select 1 lb ($\frac{1}{2}$ kg) young rou rou leaves. Remove central stalk. Chop 2 medium sized onions. Mash contents of a 12 oz (300 g) tin corned beef, prepare 2 c coconut cream. Place alternate layers of rou rou leaves, meat and onion in a casserole, finishing with leaves. Pour over coconut cream flavoured with a little salt and chilli. Cover closely with lid or foil. Bake at 350° F for 30-40 minutes or until leaves are soft.

Variation: Add tomatoes.

100

Palusami

rou rou leaves
onion
cooked corned beef
   or prawns
thick coconut cream
Serves: 6 to 8

Remove the centre stalks from 24 young rou rou leaves. Chop 1 medium size onion. Prepare 8 oz ($\frac{1}{4}$ kg) cooked chopped corned beef or prawns. Prepare 1 c thick coconut cream.

Arrange 3 leaves crosswise on top of each other; making sure that each leaf overlaps the hole left by the stalk. Leaves must be top side up.

Hold the leaves in the palm of the hand so that a cup is formed. Place $\frac{1}{8}$ of meat or prawns and chopped onion in the "cup". Add 2 T coconut cream. Fold the leaves over the filling to make a little "parcel". Attach ends with a toothpick. Wrap each parcel in cooking foil or a wilted banana leaf. Repeat this 8 more times. Place parcels in dish and bake at 300°–350° F for 30 to 40 minutes.

Preparation of banana leaf:
Using a sharp knife remove about $\frac{1}{2}$ the vein leading into the stalk of a young undamaged banana leaf. Hold the leaf over a flame or hot plate until it starts to wilt. The leaf will become quite pliable. Banana leaves may be used in place of foil or cooking paper.

Corned jellied tongue

corned tongue
bay leaf
peppercorns
cloves
onion
carrot
mint
Serves: 6 to 8

Soak 1 corned tongue in cold water for 5–6 hours. Change water and bring to a boil with 1 bay leaf, 5 peppercorns, 2 cloves, 1 medium onion quartered and 1 carrot sliced. Simmer for 2 to 3 hours or until easily pierced with a fork.

Turn off heat and let cool until easily handled. Transfer tongue to a platter. Remove skin, root and any small bones. Slit tongue in half lengthwise. Chop 1 T mint finely. Mix with 1 T broth. Press tongue into a container in which it will fit snugly. Pour mint sauce over meat. Place plate (slightly smaller than container) on top and weight with something heavy. Refrigerate overnight. Turn out and slice. *Note:* If tongue is packed into container firmly enough there is no need for additional gelatine and broth to be added other than the mint sauce as there will be enough natural juice and gelatine present to gelatinize the tongue.

Roti enchiladas

onion
garlic
oil
tinned tomatoes
tomato paste
water
sugar
vinegar
beef boullion cube
green pepper
chilli powder
cinnamon
ground cloves

Sauce

Sauté 1 medium sized chopped onion and 1 crushed clove of garlic in 2 T oil. Add 1 small tin of tomatoes (16 oz or $\frac{1}{2}$ kg), 1 small tin tomato paste (5 oz or 125 g), 1 c water, 3 T sugar, 1 T vinegar, 1 beef cube, $\frac{1}{4}$ c chopped green pepper, 2 level T chilli powder, $\frac{1}{2}$ t cinnamon and $\frac{1}{4}$ t cloves. Simmer for 45 minutes or until thick. Sieve or purée in blender.
Note: This is a Fijian version of a Mexican dish. In the original, tortillas are filled with a meat mixture and covered with a spicy chilli sauce. In this recipe we have used roti instead of tortillas.
Variation: This is a very hot sauce. Reduce chilli to $\frac{1}{2}$–1 T for a milder flavour.

Meat

garlic
onion
oil
minced beef
water
oregano
salt
cumin

Chop 1 clove garlic and 1 small onion finely; sauté in 2 T oil. Add 1 lb ($\frac{1}{2}$ kg) minced beef and 2 c water. Season with 1 t dried oregano, 1 t salt and a dash of ground cumin. Simmer until almost dry. If oregano is not available, add 1 t chopped rosemary.

Assemble roti

roti
sauce
onion
meat
Cheddar cheese
Serves: 6 to 8

Prepare 6–8 Rotis (p. 148). Spread a little sauce on each, then add 2 T each chopped onion, grated Cheddar cheese and meat mixture. Roll up, cut in half and place in a large casserole dish.
Pour the remaining sauce over rolls. Sprinkle liberally with grated cheese. Bake in a moderate oven 350° F for 35 to 40 minutes or until cheese is melted and the casserole is heated through.

Fijian lasagne

Have $\frac{3}{4}$ lb (about 350 g) lasagne noodles on hand or prepare special noodles as directed.

Special lasagne noodles

eggs
water
salt
rou rou or spinach
flour
oil

Beat 3 eggs with 3 T water, $1\frac{1}{2}$ t salt and 2 T cooked puréed rou rou or spinach. Sift 3 c flour into a bowl. Make a well in the centre. Slowly pour in mixture, stirring with a wooden spoon until a kneadable consistency is reached. Place on a floured board and knead well. Cover with a damp cloth and leave for 15 to 20 minutes. Rub a little oil on the hands and continue kneading until the dough is smooth and elastic. Roll out dough on slightly oiled surface as thinly as possible. Leave to dry for 15 to 20 minutes. Roll up like a jelly roll. Cut into 2-inch strips. Unroll onto a dry cloth. Leave to dry for 5 to 6 hours or overnight. It is then ready to be used or may be stored in an airtight container for future use.

Preparation of lasagne

mince
onion
garlic
oil
tinned tomatoes

Brown 1 lb ($\frac{1}{2}$ kg) mince, 1 c finely chopped onion and 1 crushed clove garlic in 2 T oil. Add 1 large tin tomatoes (1 lb 4 oz) (about 500 g), 1 tin tomato paste (5 oz or 125 g), $\frac{1}{2}$ c water, 1 t salt, $\frac{1}{4}$ t cayenne pepper, $\frac{1}{2}$ t

103

tomato paste
water
salt
cayenne pepper
basil
marjoram
bay leaf
rou rou
Cheddar cheese
cream cheese
Parmesan cheese
lasagne noodles
Serves: 8 to 10

basil, $\frac{1}{4}$ t marjoram and 1 bay leaf to the mince. Simmer over low heat for 2 hours or until thick and smooth.
Shred and cook $\frac{1}{4}$ lb ($\frac{1}{4}$ kg) rou rou, grate $\frac{1}{2}$ lb ($\frac{1}{4}$ kg) Cheddar cheese, cream $\frac{1}{2}$ lb ($\frac{1}{4}$ kg) cream cheese and have on hand $\frac{1}{4}$ c grated Parmesan cheese.
Place $\frac{3}{4}$ lb (300 g) purchased or special lasagne noodles in boiling salted water and cook for 10 minutes. Drain and lay on cloth to dry for 20 minutes. Spread cream cheese on dried noodles.
Place a little meat sauce in the bottoms of two 8-inch square tins or 1 very large casserole dish. Follow this with a crosswise layer of noodles, meat sauce, Cheddar cheese and Parmesan cheese. Repeat layers of noodles, sauce and cheese, placing noodles lengthwise and then crosswise, twice more.
Finally add the last and fourth layer of lasagne lengthwise, followed by rou rou and the last of the sauce and cheese.
Bake in 350° F oven for $1\frac{1}{2}$ to 2 hours.
This is ideal for a buffet dinner as all preparation may be done ahead of time and the casserole frozen or refrigerated until the time of baking. It is also excellent cold or reheated.

Beef kovu

Follow the same recipe as for Turtle p. 87.

Beef kovu dinner

A good recipe for tough beef.

stewing steak
onions
sweet potato or
   cooking bananas
tomatoes

Cut $1\frac{1}{2}$ lb ($\frac{3}{4}$ kg) stewing steak into cubes. Slice 2 medium sized onions, 2 c sweet potato or cooking bananas, and 3–4 tomatoes. Prepare 2 c coconut cream.
Combine all ingredients and sprinkle with

104

coconut cream
salt
banana leaves
Serves: 4–6

$1\frac{1}{2}$ t salt. Wrap in wilted banana leaves, tie up and steam 2–2$\frac{1}{2}$ hours.

Beef curry

onion
chillies
oil
cumin seed
blade steak
curry powder
turmeric
salt
green ginger
garlic
tomato
potato
Serves: 4

Finely chop $\frac{1}{2}$ medium-size onion and 2–3 chillies. Sauté in $\frac{1}{4}$ c oil with 1 t cumin seed until onion is golden. Add 1 lb cubed blade steak, 2 T curry powder, 1 t turmeric and $1\frac{1}{2}$ t salt. Cover and cook for 10 minutes, stirring occasionally. Finely chop 1 inch piece of green ginger and 4 garlic cloves. Add to curry. Cover and cook for 5 minutes more. Stir in 1 medium chopped tomato and 1 c cubed raw potato. Simmer until potato is soft.
Serve with rice, puris, rotis, etc.
Variation: Add 1 c chopped okra or eggplant.

Cold meat pie

beef mince
veal
pork sausage meat
onion
potato
egg
water
nutmeg
ginger
salt
chicken bouillion
 cubes
short crust pastry
milk
Serves: 8

Blend 1 lb ($\frac{1}{2}$ kg) fine mince, 8 oz ($\frac{1}{4}$ kg) minced veal and 8 oz ($\frac{1}{4}$ kg) pork sausage meat together. Grate or mince 6 oz (150 g) onion and 8 oz ($\frac{1}{4}$ kg) raw potato. Blend into meat mixture with 2 well beaten eggs and $\frac{1}{2}$ c water. Season with $\frac{1}{4}$ t nutmeg, $\frac{1}{4}$ t ginger, 2 t salt and 2 chicken stock cubes. Place in a saucepan and cook over low heat for 10 minutes stirring frequently.
Note: This is a very thick mixture. Allow to cool.
Prepare sufficient short crust pastry for a two-crusted 9-inch pie (about 8 oz, $\frac{1}{4}$ kg). Spread meat mixture firmly and evenly in a 9-inch lined pie plate. Cover with top crust and seal edges using the tines of a fork. Brush with milk. Bake in 375° F oven for 40–50 minutes.
Serve well chilled with tomato sauce and relishes of your own choice.

105

Kebabs

Delicious Kebabs can be made out of any tender meat, combined with a variety of vegetables. To make kebabs, cut meat into pieces approximately 1 inch square and about $\frac{1}{4}$ inch thick. The meat may be marinated in a flavoured sauce, see p. 98, but this is not necessary. Thread alternate pieces of meat, sliced onions, green pepper (capsicum), eggplant or mushrooms on a skewer, or coconut sasa (coconut leaf rib). Brush with oil or melted butter. Season well. Grill over hot coals or under an electric griller.

Kebabs should be served with rice and preferably with a good rich sauce made from wine, tomato, soy sauce and ginger or peanuts.

Sate with peanut sauce

A famous Indonesian dish.

pork, beef or chicken	Cut 1½ lb (¾ kg) tender pork, beef or chicken into pieces 1 inch × ¼ inch thick.
coconut cream	Prepare a marinade from 1 c coconut cream, 2 t soy sauce, 1 T sugar, 1 T lemon juice, 2 crushed garlic cloves, 1 small finely chopped onion and a little salt. Marinate meat for several hours. Thread onto skewers and grill over charcoal or under electric griller.
soy sauce	
sugar	
lemon juice	
garlic	
onion	
salt	
Serves: 6	Serve with Peanut Sauce (p. 181) and rice.

Meat balls with sweet and sour sauce

minced beef	Re-mince 1½ lb (¾ kg) minced beef with 1 medium size onion. Blend in 2 eggs, ¼ t pepper, ¼ t grated nutmeg, 1 t salt and 1 small crushed garlic clove. Form into small balls and chill for at least 1 hour. Fry in 2 T oil until brown and cooked through. Drain and keep warm.
onion	
eggs	
pepper	
nutmeg	
salt	
garlic	
oil	Prepare sweet and sour sauce by combining ¾ c sugar, 1 c vinegar, 1 c water, ½ inch crushed green ginger and 1 crushed garlic clove. Bring to a boil. Stir in 1 T cornflour and 1 t salt which has been mixed to a paste with ¼ c water. Simmer until thick.
sugar	
vinegar	
water	
green ginger	
cornflour	

106

green pepper	Finally add 1 c coarsely chopped green
pineapple or	pepper, 2 c cubed pineapple or pawpaw
pawpaw	and meat balls.
Serves: 6	Simmer for 5 minutes and serve.

Pork

Good pork is available in many tropical countries. The pig thrives in a hot climate when well fed and raised in a clean environment.

Good pork should not contain a great deal of fat. Hams and shoulders should be covered with $\frac{1}{2}$–$\frac{3}{4}$ inch of fat.

Pork should be hung for at least four days before using. This aids the tenderizing process. Fresh pork may be stored on the lower shelf of the refrigerator and turned daily.

Pork may be prepared in numerous ways. It is equally good roasted, boiled or cut into fine shreds and sautéd with vegetables, as in many Chinese and Japanese recipes.

Because of its bland flavour the right choice of seasonings is very important in pork cookery.

Fresh pork or ham may be glazed with honey, golden syrup or brown sugar.

Roast leg of pork (Chinese way)

leg of pork	Ask the butcher to score skin with the point
water	of a sharp knife at $\frac{1}{4}$ inch intervals an
salt	8–10 lb (4–5 kg) leg of pork. Pour a kettle
Serves: as desired	of boiling water over the leg. When dry, rub with salt, put the pork in the oven at 500° F and cook for 1 hour. Reduce the heat to 300° F and cook for 2–2$\frac{1}{2}$ hours, or until done.

Roast honey pork

leg of pork	Score a 4–5 lb (2–2$\frac{1}{2}$ kg) leg of pork by
green ginger	cutting through the skin and fat in a criss-
oil	cross fashion. Run a knife between the
ground ginger	skin and the meat to form a pocket. Grate
salt	1 T of green ginger finely and spread
honey	evenly into pocket. Mix 2 T oil, 2 t ground
Serves: 8 to 10	ginger and 2 t salt together. Thoroughly

107

brush leg of pork with oil mixture and place in oven. Brush with the remaining oil periodically while cooking. Allow 30 minutes cooking time per pound, or 60 minutes per kg. Glaze pork 15 minutes before it is done by pouring ½ c honey over it.
Delicious with candied carrots and onion dalo cakes.
Variation: Pineapple juice may be used in place of honey.

Glazed pickled pork

leg of pickled pork
water
mixed fresh herbs
cloves
lemon juice
brown sugar
tinned or fresh
pineapple or
crystallized
cherries
Serve: as desired

Wrap an 8–10 lb (4–5 kg) leg of pickled pork in a cloth and place in a large pot or washing boiler. Cover with plenty of water. Add a bunch of fresh herbs or 2 t dried mixed herbs and 2 t cloves. Bring to the boil and simmer for 2–2½ hours. Take out, remove cloth and peel off the skin. This should pull away easily if the pork is sufficiently cooked. Score the pork with the point of a knife crossways and diagonally. Decorate with whole cloves and pour ½ c lemon juice over it. Sprinkle generously with sugar. Bake ¾–1 hour at 350° F or until golden brown. Remove and decorate by inserting pieces of pineapple or crystallized cherries into the skin. Bake a further 10–15 minutes, being careful to avoid burning the fruit. Serve hot or cold.

Philippino pork

loin of pork
water
sugar

Finely score the skin of 4–5 lb (2–2½ kg) loin of pork using a sharp knife. Pour over a kettle of boiling water. Bake at 500° F for ½ hour until brown. Pour sweet and sour sauce over pork. Bake at 300° F for 2½ hours.

Sauce

vinegar
green ginger
garlic

Combine 2 c sugar, 1 c vinegar, 1 c water, 1 t crushed green ginger and 1 t chopped garlic. Add 1 T cornflour and 1 t salt mixed

cornflour
salt
Serves: 6

to a paste with ¼ c water. Stir, bring to boil and simmer until thick.

Sweet and sour pork

boned pork

Remove the bones and excess fat from a piece of pork large enough to yield 1½ lb (¾ kg) meat. Cut into ½ inch cubes.

Sauce

cornflour
sugar
white vinegar
water
sweet sherry
soy sauce
carrot
green pepper
water chestnuts
pickled onions
pineapple
oil

Combine ⅓ T cornflour, ⅓ c sugar, ⅓ c white vinegar, ⅓ c water, 1 t sweet sherry and 1 T soy sauce, in a saucepan. Cook over medium heat stirring constantly until sauce is thick and smooth. Turn off heat and put the sauce aside.

Slice 1 large carrot diagonally, chop ⅓ c green pepper into ¼ inch pieces, slice ⅓ c water chestnuts and section 3 pickled onions into eights. Cube 3 slices of tinned or fresh pineapple.

Heat 2 T oil in frying pan. Add carrots and stir fry for 5 minutes. Add green pepper and water chestnuts; continue cooking and stirring for another 5 minutes. Stir in onion and pineapple; remove from heat and add to sauce.

Pork

eggs
flour
salt
sweet sherry
oil
Serves: 6

Mix 2 eggs, 6 T flour, 2 t salt and 2 t sweet sherry together. Fold in pork cubes. Heat 2 c or more of oil in pan until very hot.

Fry pork; 6 pieces at a time to ensure their cooking quickly and thoroughly. Drain and keep warm.

Serve on a large platter with cooked rice. Pour over sauce just before serving. Do not apply sauce ahead of time as the pork will go soggy.

Pork in sour cream

lean pork chops
*   or steak*
seasoned flour
oil
sour cream
lemon juice
salt
dried thyme
sugar
water
Serves: 5 to 6

Trim the fat from 1½ lb (¾ kg) chops or steak. Cut into servings. Roll in seasoned flour. Brown in about ½ c hot oil. Place in casserole dish. Combine 4 oz sour cream, 2 T lemon juice, 1 t salt, 1 t dried thyme and 1 t sugar. Pour over pork. Add sufficient water to cover meat. Cover with lid and bake at 350° F for 1 hour or until tender.

Barbecue pork belly (spare ribs)

pork belly
seasoned flour
oil
onion
tomato sauce
water
salt
monosodium
*   glutamate*
garlic salt
onion salt
Worcestershire
*   sauce*
vinegar
sugar
dry mustard
paprika
Serves: 8

Cut 4 lb (2 kg) pork belly into serving pieces. Dredge with seasoned flour and fry in hot oil until golden. Place in a large casserole dish. Cover and bake in 375° F oven for 1½ hours. Remove from oven and drain off excess fat. Prepare barbecue sauce of 1 c sliced onion, 1 c tomato sauce (ketchup), 1 c water, 2 t salt, 1 t monosodium glutamate, 1 t garlic salt, 1 t onion salt, 2 T Worcestershire sauce, ¼ c vinegar, ¼ c sugar, 2 t dry mustard and 1 t paprika. Pour half of the sauce over pork, cover and return to oven. Bake for a further ½ hour. Remove cover and baste with remaining sauce every few minutes for the next hour. Serve with boiled rice.
Note: 1 small chopped clove garlic may replace 1 t garlic salt.

110

Chicken

Like other meats the quality of chicken depends on the age of the bird and the time allowed for maturing. Village raised chicken of unknown age should be matured for at least 4 days on the lower shelf of the refrigerator. Frozen chickens obtained from a reliable dealer may be used when defrosted.

To test the age of the chicken; press the end of the breast bone. If it is hard, the chicken is old and it should be steamed, boiled, stewed or cooked slowly in a casserole. A pliable end of the breast bone indicates a chicken young enough for roasting or frying.

To ensure that chicken is tender we recommend the following procedures:

1. Cut the chicken into pieces and marinate for 4 to 5 hours in a basic lemon marinade of $\frac{1}{4}$ c lemon juice, $\frac{1}{2}$ crushed garlic clove, $\frac{1}{4}$ c oil, $\frac{1}{2}$ t salt and pepper.

   Variations:
   1. Use the preceding ingredients but replace the lemon juice with $\frac{1}{2}$ c crushed fresh pineapple or prepare the lemon marinade and add $\frac{1}{2}$ c finely chopped ripe pawpaw or replace lemon juice with white wine.
   2. Cut the chicken into pieces and marinate for 4 to 5 hours in $\frac{1}{8}$ c soy sauce, $\frac{1}{4}$ c salad oil, 2 t finely chopped onion and 1 t crushed green ginger.
   3. Use the basic recipe but replace the lemon juice with a dry red or white wine.

How to roast a chicken

Choose a fat bird of 5–9 months in age and weighing 3–5 lb ($1\frac{1}{2}$–$2\frac{1}{4}$ kg). Rub inside the cavity with salt and any other desired flavour such as garlic, lemon, or rosemary. Fill cavity with stuffing or insert onion or a bunch of herbs. Truss the bird and rub with oil or melted butter.

Place breast down, in a baking dish and put in an oven at 325–350° F. Allow 24–30 minutes per pound ($\frac{1}{2}$ kg) for smaller birds. For heavier birds 4–5 lb (2–$2\frac{1}{2}$ kg) 20–25 minutes per pound ($\frac{1}{2}$ kg) is sufficient. Stuffed birds take longer to cook— allow 35–40 minutes per pound ($\frac{1}{2}$ kg).

111

When half cooked, turn breast up and finish roasting. Baste frequently with drippings from the pan.

Lemon garlic roast chicken

chicken
garlic
lemon juice
salt
pepper
Serves: 6

Rub a 5 lb (2½ kg) trussed chicken with a cut clove of garlic, inside cavity and outside. Pour ½ c lemon juice over chicken. Sprinkle with salt and pepper. Roast at 325° F for about 1½ hours—or until the juice runs clear when leg is pierced with a skewer.

Roast chicken with rosemary

chicken
rosemary
butter
Serves: 6

Put a sprig of fresh rosemary in the cavity of a 5 lb (2½ kg) bird. Rub the skin with crushed rosemary. Pour over a little melted butter. Roast at 325° F.

Roast chicken eastern style

garlic
green ginger
soy sauce
oil
chicken
Serves: 6

Select a 4–5 lb (2–2½ kg) bird. Crush 1 garlic clove and 2 t green ginger. Mix with 1 T soy sauce and ¼ c oil. These ingredients are most easily combined in a blender. Put a little of the marinade in the cavity and pour the rest over the chicken. Bake at 350° F, basting several times.
Variation: Use half cooking oil and half sesame oil. Serve with fried pineapple pieces and a Hot Rice Salad.

Spiced chicken

chicken
pepper
ground ginger
cardamom pods
salt
turmeric
onion
yoghurt
cream
Serves: 6

Prick the skin of a 5 lb (2½ kg) chicken with a fork. Rub well with a mixture of 1 t ground pepper and 1½ t ground ginger. Truss bird and place in oven at 350° F for 10 minutes. Pound 3 cardamom pods in a bowl. Add 1 t salt, 2 t ground turmeric, 3 small onions finely chopped, 1 c yoghurt and 1 c cream. Pour sauce over chicken and bake for 1½ hours or until tender. Baste frequently with sauce. Extra sauce may be placed in a bowl or sauceboat.

112

PUMPKIN

PAWPAW

DURUKA

Chicken curry

chicken
dry onion
oil
fennel seeds
cloves
cardamom pods
cinnamon sticks
curry leaves
green ginger
garlic
turmeric
chilli powder
curry powder
salt
water
coriander sprigs
Serves: 6

Cut 2 lb (1 kg) boned chicken into 2 inch cubes. Chop 1 medium size onion. Heat 3 T oil in pan. When hot add 1 t fennel seeds, 3 cloves, 5 cardamom pods and 5 small sticks of cinnamon. Stir fry until seeds are golden. Add chopped onion and 1 stem curry leaves (tejpati). Stir fry for a couple of minutes more. Add $\frac{1}{2}$ t chopped green ginger and 3 chopped garlic cloves. Cook for 3 minutes. Add chicken followed by 1 t turmeric powder, 2 t chilli powder and 2 t curry powder; add 1 t salt or to taste. Cook slowly for 10 minutes. Add 2 c water or sufficient to half cover. Cover and cook until tender. Add 2 coriander sprigs for flavour. Remove from heat and serve. If desired remove whole spice before serving.

Chicken rou rou casserole

chicken
lemon juice
seasoned flour
oil
thick coconut cream
salt
pepper
chilli (optional)
rou rou
onion
tomato
Serves: 6

Cut 2 lb (1 kg) boned chicken into 1 inch pieces. Marinate in juice of 1 lemon and $\frac{1}{4}$ c oil seasoned with salt and pepper for several hours. Drain, then roll in seasoned flour. Heat $\frac{1}{4}$ c oil and fry until golden brown.
Prepare 2 c thick coconut cream. Season with 1 t salt, $\frac{1}{4}$ t pepper and 1 finely chopped chilli (optional).
Wash approximately $1\frac{1}{2}$ lb ($\frac{3}{4}$ kg) rou rou leaves. Remove the stems and coarse veins. Finely chop 2 medium size onions.
Place a layer of leaves in casserole, cover with chicken pieces and sprinkle with onion. Pour a little of the coconut cream over the chicken.
Repeat layers, making sure that the leaves are used for the last layer. Slice 2 or 3 medium size tomatoes and place on top of leaves.

H

Cover casserole and bake for 40 to 50 minutes at 350° F.
Serve with wedges of lemon.

Chicken lolo suvu

Preparation of dhal

Arahar dhal
water

Soak 1½ c (¾ lb or 300 g) Arahar dhal or split peas in water to cover overnight. Wash and add 2 c water and bring to boil. Simmer until soft and mushy. Sieve. Refrigerate until required.

Preparation of chicken

chicken
water
garlic
salt
green ginger
onion
butter
Madras curry
  powder
turmeric
tinned tomatoes
chicken stock cubes

Section 4½ lb (2½ kg) chicken, removing flesh from back and breasts. Leave flesh on legs, wings, etc. Prepare stock using back, breast and neck along with 2½ c water. Strain off stock. Reduce to 1 c by boiling. Reserve.
Mash 10 cloves garlic with enough salt to take up moisture. This should yield 1 rounded T garlic plus salt.
Mash sufficient green ginger to yield 1 T. Chop 1½ c onion finely.
Melt ⅓ c butter in a large frying pan. Add onions and fry until golden. Stir in 2 T plus 2 t Madras curry powder, 2 t ground turmeric, prepared garlic and ginger.
Cook for 1 minute. Stir in chicken pieces and fry until brown. Add 1 small tin mashed tomatoes (8 oz or ¼ kg), 1 c prepared stock and 2 chicken stock cubes.
Simmer until just tender. Remove from heat and refrigerate until next day to allow flavour to fully develop.
Do not combine Dhal with Chicken until ready to use.

114

Day of dinner

coconut cream
onions
oil
rice
Serves: 10

Prepare 1 c very thick coconut cream. Thinly slice 5 large onions. Fry in the minimum amount of oil until slightly golden and transparent. Drain well on paper. Place on fresh paper and put in a very low oven to dry until crisp. Keep warm until ready to serve.
Prepare 1 lb ($\frac{1}{2}$ kg) white fluffy rice.

Assemble Chicken lolo suvu

Heat chicken thoroughly $\frac{1}{2}$ hour before serving. Stir in dhal and continue stirring until a smooth mixture is achieved. 5 minutes before serving, add coconut cream. Do not allow mixture to boil after coconut cream has been added as fat will separate. If a more soup-like consistency is desired more chicken broth or thick coconut cream may be added.
Serve Chicken Lolo Suvu with rice topped with dry onions.

Fruits and Desserts

Fruit Chart

Variety	Selection	Storage	Preparation and Uses
AVOCADO	Fully developed green. May be picked green and left to ripen. Ripe when soft to touch. Some varieties turn brown when ripe.	When ripe keep in refrigerator. Ripe fruit may be deep frozen whole in skin.	The cut fruit turns black very quickly. To prevent this sprinkle with lemon or lime juice or vinegar. Prepare Guacamole Dip (p. 35). Use in cocktails as in Caviar Avocado (p. 37). Prepare Moulded Avocado Salad (p. 38). Prepare Avocado Sauce (p. 39) and serve Avocado Soup (p. 44). Use in desserts in Avocado Honey Lime (p. 124), Avocado Soursop Fool (p. 124) or in Avocado Chocolate Cream (p. 128).
BANANA (LONG EATING)	Fully developed fruit. No distinct ridges down sides. Pale greenish yellow to deep yellow in colour.	Hang bunches in cool dark place. Keep fruit on racks. Do not put in refrigerator. Keeps 2–3 days.	Raw as a fruit in Tropical Fruit Salad (p. 125). or Glazed Fruit Trio (p. 126), in jellies as desserts or in ice creams and mashed in Banana Lote (p. 127). Baked in coconut cream or lemon sauce. Prepare Banana Orange Pie (p. 132) or Banana Tea Bread (p. 151). In jam as in Fruit Salad Jam (p. 175). Use raw in Banana Radish Dressing (p. 51) or in Spiced Banana and Kumala Salad (p. 55). Prepare Banana and Bacon Hors d'Oeuvres (p. 29).

	Selection	Storage	Uses
CUMQUATS	Firm yellow orange fruit.	On racks—keeps several days	Excellent in jam and marmalade. May be used to make pickles.
GRANADILLA	Pale yellow green fruit. Slightly soft.	On racks. Lasts 1–2 days depending on ripeness.	Cut in half, remove pulp and peel skin. Cut flesh into cubes. Use raw or cook in syrup. Strain seeds and serve juice with cubed flesh.
GRAPEFRUIT	Pale greenish yellow firm fruit.	On racks—keeps a week.	Serve raw as a breakfast fruit. Flavour with sherry and serve as an appetiser. Combine with avocado to form a cocktail. Use in fruit salad as in Sherry Fruit Salad (p. 124). Prepare Citrus Marmalade (p 176).
GUAVA	Large greenish yellow fruit. Must be fairly firm.	On racks. Keeps several days.	Peel, cut in half and scoop out seeds. Use shell raw or cooked in fruit salads. Cook shells in syrup with a little lemon juice. Cook seeds and pulp, sieve and use guava purée as a fruit sauce or ice cream or a cold soufflé. Prepare Guava Jelly (p. 175) or Guava Gelato (p. 130).
LADIES FINGERS (SHORT EATING)	Fully developed fruit. No distinct ridges down sides. Pale greenish yellow to deep yellow in colour.	Hang bunches in cool dark place. Keep fruit on racks. Do not put in refrigerator. Keeps 4–5 days.	Use similarly to bananas. Has a tart flavour. Carries well. Good for picnics.
LIMES	Green and greenish yellow fruit.	On racks—keeps a week.	Use juice in drinks and to flavour many sweet and savoury dishes in place of lemons. Excellent in pickles as in Hot Spicy Lime Pickle (p. 182) and Plain Lime Pickle (p. 182).
MANDARINS	Greenish orange	On racks—keeps a week	Use juice in drinks. Makes excellent jelly. Combine in fruit salad. A good picnic fruit.

Variety	Selection	Storage	Preparation and Uses
MANGOES	Firm yellow or orange coloured fruit. Avoid fruit with turpentine smell.	On racks in cool dark place for 2 days.	Peel ripe fruit and use raw in salads. Add sugar or a syrup and use as dessert. Cook half ripe fruit in syrup. Cook ripe or half ripe fruit in water and sugar and make a purée for ice cream, or a soufflé or prepare Mango Mousse (p. 130). Peel green mangoes and make Jelly (p. 175). Use green mango in Fruit Sauce or Ketchup (p. 179). Prepare Mango Jam (p. 176). Use half ripe mangoes in Basic Mango Chutney (p. 177).
ORANGES	Greenish yellow	On racks in cool dark place—keeps a week.	Many tropical varieties have coarse fibre dividing the segments. Cut segments out with a sharp knife and remove before including in salads, etc. Makes good drinks although rather tart in flavour. Use in Citrus Marmalade (p. 176). Prepare Orange Banana Pie (p. 132).
PASSIONFRUIT (HARD YELLOW SKIN)	Yellow to brownish yellow. Sweet fruit with slightly wrinkled skin.	On racks. Keeps several days.	Cut in half, scoop out pulp, use in ice cream and soufflé recipes. Serve in half shell with sugar. Prepare Tropical Fruit Salad (p. 125). Strain, sweeten with sugar and use juice to make drinks.
PASSIONFRUIT or BELL APPLE (soft skin)	Deep orange colour. Smooth skin.	On racks. Keeps several days.	Use as for passionfruit but add lime or lemon and additional sugar to develop flavour.

PAWPAW (PAPAYA)	Yellow to orange coloured fruit. Must be firm.	On racks. Keeps 2–3 days when half ripe. Ripe fruit lasts 1–2 days.	Cut in halves or quarters, remove seeds, flavour with lime or lemon. Excellent served raw as breakfast fruit. Cut into cubes and add to salads or fruit cocktails. Prepare Glazed Fruit Trio (p. 126). Cooked pawpaw may be used in jellies. Raw fruit stops gelatine from setting. Prepare Brandied Pawpaw Whip (p. 128).
PINEAPPLE	Yellow to orange colour. Must be firm all over.	Store on racks. Keeps 2–3 days.	Peel off outer skin. Remove black eyes by cutting a wedge $\frac{1}{4}$ inch deep diagonally across fruit. Serve raw in slices or cubes. Add to salads of all types, as in Tropical Bean Salad (p. 57) or Tropical Fruit Salad (p. 125). Served cooked with pork and steak, grilled, or fried until golden brown. Prepare Pineapple Lamb Chops (p. 90), or Steak and Pineapple (p. 99). Feature in desserts as Minted Pineapple (p. 125) or Pineapple Lote (p. 127). Use in pickles and chutney. Do not use in gelatine mixtures unless cooked.
POMELO	Yellow green fruit	On racks—keeps a week.	A mild flavoured grapefruit type citrus. Treat as for grapefruit. Excellent as breakfast fruit and in fruit cocktails.
ROCK MELON	Greenish yellow round fruit, just firm to the touch.	As pomelo. Cover well in refrigerator as flavour permeates other food.	Cut in halves or wedges. Remove seeds, use as breakfast or lunch fruit or as appetiser at dinner, use in fruit salads. Flavour with lemon, ginger, and sugar.
ROSE APPLE (KAVIKA)	Pale pinkish yellow.	On racks. Keeps several days.	Best eaten raw. May be peeled and included in fruit salads. A favourite children's fruit.

Variety	Selection	Storage	Preparation and Uses
SOURSOP	Green but soft fruit.	On racks. Lasts 1–2 days.	Cut in half and scoop out soft flesh. Sieve to remove fibre and seeds. Use purée to prepare drinks, ice cream and cold desserts such as Avocado Soursop Fool (p. 124). Combines well with banana and avocado. Makes an excellent fresh fruit sauce to serve with desserts. Prepare Soursop Jam (p. 176).
WATER MELON	Hard greenish yellow colour. Should have hollow sound when thumped.	On racks. Keeps 1–2 weeks.	Chill, cut in slices, serve raw. Remove seeds, cube or make balls and add to fruit salads. Cut longitudinally, scoop out pink centre, combine with other fruits. Serve fruit salad in shells. Flavour with lemon, port wine, ginger.

Desserts and In-betweens

A well chosen dessert should provide a perfect ending to a meal. The choice of dessert is important. The flavour and texture should provide contrast to earlier dishes. For example, do not have a chocolate cream pie if cream soup is being served in the first course. Desserts vary in ingredients and it is wise to serve a simple fruit salad if rich recipes are used in earlier courses.

The desserts given in this section have been chosen because of their good flavour and their comparative ease of preparation. The greater number may be prepared ahead of time and stored in the refrigerator.

We would like to draw your attention to different ways in which raw fruits may be used to make unusual fruit salads. Fruit makes a particularly good end to a tropical lunch or dinner menu.

Flaming fruit

Fruits such as tinned peaches, ripe mangoes, pineapple and ripe bananas may be served in this way.

Canned fruit must be well drained.

Raw fruit should be first dipped in sugar. Place fruit in a warm dish or chafing dish and leave in a warm oven for a few minutes. Heat brandy in a spoon or ladle over a candle. Pour over hot fruit and light with a match at the table. Remember that the brandy will not light unless it is warm.

Raw fruit in interesting ways

Vary fruit salads in the following ways:

Mint fruit salad

Chop a handful of fresh mint. Pour boiling water over this and leave to cool. Use the mint water to make a sugar syrup to pour over the fruit.

Lemon fruit salad

Make a lemon flavoured sugar syrup for fruit.

123

Tomato fruit salad

Add chopped tomato to the fruit salad mixture.

Sherry fruit salad

Serve grapefruit pieces or water melon balls flavoured with sherry and well chilled.

Melon port wine

Serve rock melon balls well chilled in port wine.

Ginger fruit salad

Add chopped crystallised ginger to rock melon, pineapple or pawpaw fruit salads.

Avocado, honey, lime

Mash or sieve ripe avocado till creamy. Flavour with lime juice and honey or sugar. Mix with a little whipped cream and serve as a sauce with other fruit or with ice cream.

Avocado, soursop fool

Combine equal quantities of sieved avocado with sieved soursop. Add $\frac{1}{4}$ quantity whipped cream and sugar to taste, place in individual glasses, chill and serve as a fruit fool.

Fruit salad and toasted coconut

Arrange sliced fruits around vanilla ice cream. Top the ice cream with toasted coconut or pass this in a dish.

Flavoured cream and fruit salad

Serve fruit salads with flavoured whipped cream. 2 t of a liqueur such as Crème de Menthe, grenadine or curaçao added to a cup of whipped cream is delicious. Sweeten cream with icing sugar and flavour with vanilla essence or lemon essence and a little grated lemon rind. Chopped nuts, crystallised ginger or glacé cherries may be added to cream.

Minted pineapple

pineapple
lime juice
crème de menthe
sweetened cream
fresh mint
Serves: 6

Cut a ripe medium sized pineapple into small cubes. Sprinkle with the juice of 1 fresh lime and ½ c creme de menthe. Add extra Crème de Menthe if you prefer a stronger mint flavour. Cover and leave in the refrigerator for at least 1 hour. Serve in glasses topped with pale green sweetened cream and fresh mint leaves.

Pineapple glaze

pineapple
sugar
cointreau
ice cream
Serves: 4 to 6

Choose a pineapple, regular in shape with tufted top still on. Remove top, reserving to use as a lid. Carefully remove all flesh leaving a rind of skin and flesh about ½ inch thick. Dust the inside with 1 T sugar and sprinkle with 2 T cointreau. Chill for 2 hours.

Chop pineapple finely, mix with ice cream and fill pineapple. Place in freezer compartment of refrigerator, for at least 2 hours before serving. Serve from pineapple at the table.

Variation: If large quantities are required, a simplified method may be used.

Peel and cube pineapple. Add liqueur and sugar. Leave for 2 hours. Blend in desired quantity of ice cream and freeze in a suitable container until firm.

Tropical fruit salad

pineapple
water
pawpaw
passionfruit
sugar
crème de menthe

Wash 1 pineapple well, peel and reserve skin. Simmer skins with ½ c water for 15 minutes. Strain and put aside to cool.

Cube pineapple and just ripe (very firm) pawpaw to yield 1 c each. Carefully stir in ¼ c passionfruit. Add prepared juice, ¼ c

125

banana
Serves: 6

sugar, or to taste, and 1 t Crème de Menthe. Chill well. Just before serving add 2 large sliced bananas.

Glazed fruit trio with crumb topping
Sauce
sugar
cornflour
salt
water
egg
lemon juice
lemon rind
butter

Combine 1 c sugar, 3 T cornflour, $\frac{1}{4}$ t salt and $1\frac{1}{4}$ c water. Stir and cook over medium heat for 5 minutes or until thick and smooth. Beat 1 egg. Slowly beat in a little of the cornflour mixture, then add to remaining mixture in pan. Cook over low heat for 1 minute. Remove from stove and cool slightly. Add $\frac{1}{3}$ c lemon juice, $\frac{1}{2}$ t grated lemon rind and 2 T butter.

Fruit
pineapple
pawpaw
banana

Prepare $1\frac{1}{2}$ c cubed pineapple, $1\frac{1}{2}$ c cubed just ripe pawpaw and 1 c sliced banana. Place in bowl and pour sauce over the top. Refrigerate until thoroughly chilled and ready to serve.

Caramel crumbs
brown sugar
flour
salt
butter
Serves: 8

Mix $\frac{1}{3}$ c brown sugar, $\frac{1}{2}$ c flour, $\frac{1}{4}$ t salt and 2 T butter together. Bake in 375° F oven for 10 minutes or until crisp and golden. If crumbs stick together, roll when cool. Serve with crumbs sprinkled liberally over the top with ice cream or whipped cream. *Variation:* Use soursop juice or orange juice in place of water in sauce.

PUDDINGS
Basic lote supreme
milk
cassava (tapioca)
egg
sugar
alt
utt

Heat $2\frac{1}{2}$ c milk in double boiler. Add $\frac{3}{4}$ c finely grated tapioca (cassava), stirring constantly. Stir until thick. Cover and cook for 30 minutes or until cassava has dissolved. Beat 1 egg with $\frac{1}{2}$ c milk, add $\frac{1}{4}$ c sugar and $\frac{1}{4}$ t salt. Slowly add to pudding, stirring

126

vanilla
Serves: 6 to 8

while you do so. Cook for 2–3 minutes. Remove from heat and add 1 T butter and 1 t vanilla essence.
This dish may be served hot or cold.
Variations:
Chocolate. Increase sugar to ½ c and add ½ c cocoa with it.
Banana. Add 2 well mashed bananas with butter and vanilla.
Pineapple. Add 1 c finely chopped pineapple with butter and vanilla.
Lemon. Add 1 T grated lemon rind with sugar and egg and omit vanilla.
Coconut. Add ½ c finely grated fresh coconut with butter and vanilla.

Sponge custard pudding

butter
sugar
water
eggs
flour
lemon juice
lemon rind
milk
Serves: 4

Blend 1 T butter with ¾ c sugar. Add 1 T hot water. Beat in 2 egg yolks, 2 T flour, 2 T lemon juice and the rind from 1 large lemon. Stir in 5 fl oz (126 ml) milk.
Beat 2 egg whites until they are stiff but not dry. Fold into butter mixture.
Place in a buttered casserole dish.
Bake in a shallow pan of hot water in a 325° F oven for 1 hour or until puffy and golden. Equally good hot or cold.

Chocolate pudding

sugar
butter
egg
vanilla essence
flour
cornflour
baking powder
cocoa
milk
water
Serves: 6

Cream ½ c sugar with ¼ c butter. Add 1 beaten egg, ½ t vanilla and beat well.
Sift ¾ c flour with ¼ c cornflour, 1½ t baking powder and 3 T cocoa. Measure ½ c milk.
Fold dry ingredients alternating with cold milk into butter mixture.
Place in greased casserole dish. Mix ½ c sugar with 2 T cocoa. Sprinkle over cake mixture in casserole dish. Gently pour 1½ c boiling water over top.
Bake in a 350° F oven for 40 to 50 minutes. The top will be firm and cake-like when

127

done and a chocolate sauce will be present at the bottom.

Serve cake in dish with chocolate sauce from bottom of dish poured over the top.

Refrigerated desserts

Lemon cheese cake

sweet crumb pastry
cream cheese
egg
caster sugar
vanilla essence
reduced cream
lemon juice
fresh nutmeg
Serves: 6

Prepare 1 c Sweet Crumb Pastry (p. 147), and place in a 9 inch pie plate or in a springform pan. Chill. A springform pan makes it slightly easier to remove slices. Cream well 8 oz ($\frac{1}{4}$ kg) softened cream cheese. Add 1 egg, $\frac{1}{2}$ c caster sugar and 1 t vanilla essence. Beat for 5 minutes. Pour into prepared, chilled shell and bake in 350° F oven for 30 minutes. It will rise slightly and be firm but not brown when done. Remove and allow to cool for 5 to 10 minutes.

Beat 1 c tinned cream or thick fresh cream with 2 T lemon juice, 1 T sugar and 1 t vanilla. Spread evenly over partially cooled pie. Sprinkle with freshly grated nutmeg. Bake in a 500° F oven for 2 to 3 minutes. Remove, cool and refrigerate until ready to use.

This is similar to larger, more expensive cheese cakes but is smaller, more economical and therefore ideal for smaller families.

Avocado chocolate cream

avocado
lemon juice
sugar
ice cream
grated chocolate
Serves: 4

Peel, mash and sieve 1 large avocado. Add $\frac{1}{4}$ c sugar and $\frac{1}{4}$ c lemon juice. Place in 4 serving dishes and chill thoroughly. Just before serving add 1 large scoop of ice cream and sprinkle liberally with grated chocolate.

Brandied pawpaw whip

pawpaw
sugar

Select a ripe but firm pawpaw. Peel and remove seeds. Mash sufficient to yield $1\frac{1}{2}$ c.

128

Another luncheon or supper dish—stuffed breadfruit.

Stuffed eggplant makes a good luncheon dish.

Minted pineapple is a cool and pleasant dessert. Other fruits can be served in the same way.

Pavlova cake filled with pawpaw brandy whip.

lemon juice
gelatine
water
brandy
cream
Serves: 6

Add ¼ c lemon juice and ½ c sugar, put in saucepan. Boil for 5 minutes. Combine 2 t gelatine with 1 T water. Stir into hot fruit. Reduce fruit to a purée in a blender or by sieving. Add ½–1 T brandy.
Cool. When partially set fold in 2 c cream which has been whipped.
Serve plain or with ice cream and toasted coconut. Use as a filling for Pavlova Cake (p. 153).

Pumpkin soufflé

gelatine
water
eggs
caster sugar
rum
pumpkin
cinnamon
ginger
mace or nutmeg
lemon rind
whipped cream
Serves: 6

Soak 1 T gelatine in ¼ c water for 5 minutes. Melt over hot water. Beat 4 eggs over hot water until thick. Gradually add ⅔ c caster sugar and continue beating. Add melted gelatine, 1 T rum and 1 c cooked sieved pumpkin. Season with ½ t powdered cinnamon, ½ t ground ginger, ½ t ground mace or grated nutmeg and the rind from 1 lemon.
Remove from heat and fold in ½ pint whipped cream.
Serve well chilled.
Variation: Add ½ c mixed dried fruit to gelatine pumpkin mixture.

Wine jelly

water
sugar
cloves
cinnamon stick
lemon jelly powder
gelatine
medium sherry
lemon juice
Serves: 10 to 12

Bring 6 c water, 1 c sugar, 15 cloves and 5 sticks cinnamon (1 inch × ¼ inch) to a boil. Simmer gently for 10 minutes.
Place 1 package lemon jelly powder, 2 T gelatine, 1 c medium sherry and 2 T lemon juice in a bowl. Let stand for 5 minutes. Pour boiling syrup over gelatine mixture. Stir well until it is thoroughly dissolved and mixed. Strain.
Refrigerate until set.
Serve with cream or ice cream and fruit of your choice.
A simple, but very special dessert, excellent after a rich main course.

Frozen desserts

Mango mousse

parrot mangoes
sugar
lemon juice
gelatine
water
fresh cream
Serves: 6

Peel and slice 3 large ripe, but firm mangoes (parrot mangoes for preference). Place in saucepan with $\frac{1}{2}$ c sugar. Cook and stir over low heat for about 10 minutes or until soft. Purée and measure 1 c. Add 1 T lemon juice. Place 2 t gelatine in $\frac{1}{4}$ c cold water. Leave for 5 minutes. Dissolve gelatine mixture over low heat and then stir into purée. Allow to cool.

Whip $\frac{1}{2}$ pint (285 ml) fresh cream until stiff. Fold in cooled mango purée and place in a 1 pint (570 ml) mould. Cover with aluminium foil and place in freezer part of refrigerator. Freeze until firm.

This has a delicate mango flavour and is smooth and creamy to the palate.

Note : Any ripe mango of good flavour may be substituted for parrot mangoes.

Coconut sherbet

caster sugar
water
vanilla essence
freshly grated
  coconut
whipped cream
Serves: 6

Boil $\frac{2}{3}$ c sugar with $1\frac{1}{2}$ c water for 5 minutes. Add 2 t vanilla essence and 2 c freshly grated coconut. Remove from stove and leave to cool.

Fold in $\frac{1}{2}$ pint (285 ml) whipped cream. Freeze until mushy. Remove and beat until smooth. Freeze until firm.

Serve with a chocolate sauce or a fruit sauce made from passionfruit, guava or mango purée.

Guava gelato

milk
sugar
gelatine
water
lemon juice
guava juice

Heat 1 c milk with $\frac{1}{2}$ c sugar, stirring until sugar is dissolved. Dissolve 1 t gelatine in 1 T cold water. Add to hot milk.

Add 2 T lemon juice to 1 c guava juice. Add milk mixture while stirring vigorously. Place in freezer tray and freeze until

130

Serves: 6

mushy. Beat well and refreeze until firm. Delicious served with sliced bananas or just by itself.
Note : Preparation of guava juice. Wash and slice guavas. Weigh and add 1½ c water per lb (½ kg) fruit. Simmer for 45 minutes or until soft. Stand for 20 minutes and then strain through cheese cloth. Extra may be stored in refrigerator and used as a fruit drink.

Pies

Kumala pie (sweet potato)

basic short crust pastry
kumalas
salted water
evaporated milk
eggs
sugar
lemon juice
nutmeg
Serves: 6 to 8

Prepare 9 inch or 2 small 8 inch pie shells ready for the oven, but do not prick pastry. Peel and boil in salted water sufficient kumalas to yield 1 c cooked, sieved pulp. 1 large kumala should be sufficient for this. Beat together 1⅔ c evaporated milk, 2 eggs, ¾ c sugar, 1 c sieved kumala and 1 T lemon juice. Carefully place in unbaked pie shell. Sprinkle the top with a little freshly grated nutmeg and sugar.

Bake in 450° F oven for first 10 minutes. Reduce heat to 325° F (moderate) and continue baking for a further 40 to 50 minutes. It will be done when filling slightly puffs up and a knife inserted in the middle comes out clean.

Chill pie thoroughly and serve. It is very nice by itself or with ice cream or whipped cream.

Chocolate kumala pie

kumala pie
dark chocolate
butter
icing sugar
Serves: 6 to 8

Prepare Kumala Pie ready for baking but omit sprinkling nutmeg and sugar on top. Bake and partially cool pie. Prepare the following topping. Melt ½ large bar dark chocolate (1¼ oz or 30 g) with 1 t butter in top of double boiler or heavy saucepan. Remove from heat and add 2 T boiling water and 1 c

131

sifted icing sugar. Beat until smooth and glossy. Pour over warm pie and chill well before serving.

This looks delicious and tastes even better.

Spicy pumpkin pie

basic short crust
  pastry
eggs
sugar
salt
cinnamon
nutmeg
allspice
ginger
ground cloves
evaporated milk
pumpkin
Serves: 6 to 8

This will make sufficient filling for 1 large 9 inch pie or 2 small 8 inch pies.

Prepare desired pie shells.

Beat 2 eggs. Add 1 c sugar, $\frac{1}{2}$ t salt, $1\frac{1}{2}$ t cinnamon, $\frac{1}{2}$ t nutmeg, $\frac{1}{4}$ t allspice, $\frac{1}{4}$ t ginger and $\frac{1}{4}$ t cloves. (All spices ground or grated.) Blend well.

Add $1\frac{2}{3}$ c (366 g) evaporated milk and $1\frac{1}{2}$ c sieved cooked pumpkin, stirring until smooth. Carefully pour into pie shell and bake in 375° F oven for 10 minutes. Reduce heat to 350° F and continue baking until a knife inserted comes out clean.

Delicious served hot or cold with ice cream or whipped cream.

Banana orange pie

tropical oranges
sugar
cornflour
gelatine
water
bananas
9 *inch baked*
  pie shell
Serves: 6

Peel and section sufficient tart tropical oranges (if temperate climate sweet oranges are used, sugar must be reduced) to yield $1\frac{1}{2}$ c juice and pulp. Remove all seeds. Drain easily removed juice into a small saucepan. Mix $\frac{1}{2}$ c sugar with $1\frac{1}{2}$ t cornflour. Add to orange juice and cook until thick and clear. Add remaining orange pulp. Taste to check that the mixture is not too sour. A tangy slightly sweet flavour is desired. Add a little more sugar at this time if needed.

Soak 2 t gelatine in 1 T water. Add to orange mixture and stir until dissolved.

Slice 4 medium sized bananas (roughly $1\frac{1}{2}$ c). Fold into orange mixture and refrigerate until cool and slightly firm. Pour into 9 inch baked pie shell and refrigerate until firm.

Serve with whipped cream or ice cream.

132

Tropical Baking

In many parts of the urban world baking is a dying culinary art. The housewife is too often tempted by frozen and fresh baked cakes, biscuits and scones offered by the bakeries and delicatessens. In many tropical cities these goods are either very expensive, or not available at all. If fresh rolls, pastry or cakes are to be served these must be homemade.

Baking in the tropics can be fraught with problems, unless great care is given to the careful storage of ingredients and the use of reliable recipes and techniques of preparation. Ingredients such as baking powder and dried yeast must be as fresh as possible. Always store in tightly closed tins and keep in a cool place. Keep sugar in a sealed container to prevent the absorption of moisture.

Flour, too, must be fresh and kept in a covered container so that it is free from weevils and moisture. Cake mixtures containing butter or margarine often appear very moist in hot weather and one is tempted to add flour. The moistness is due to the fat becoming soft in the heat. Extra flour could spoil the recipe.

In the following recipes we have given detailed instructions concerning the use of yeast in baking and on how to make good scones, pastry and roti. Remember that successful baking depends on following the recipe, and practising the techniques.

Bread and Rolls

Basic white bread and variations

yeast
water
milk
butter
sugar
salt
flour
oil
Yield:
   2 large loaves
     or
   2 dozen rolls

Rinse a large bowl with hot water to warm it. Add 2 level T dried yeast or 1 oz (25 g) fresh yeast and $\frac{1}{2}$ c lukewarm water. Leave to react for 5 to 10 minutes.

In the meantime mix together 1 c boiling water, 1 c milk, 2 T butter, 2 T sugar and 2 t salt. Let cool until it is lukewarm. Add to yeast mixture, stirring well.

Measure and sift 3 c flour. Beat into yeast mixture using an electric mixer or a wooden spoon. Thorough beating at this stage reduces the kneading time and results in a more uniform loaf.

Measure and sift a further 4 c flour. Add this slowly to the mixture, working in the flour with a wooden spoon until it forms a soft dough which no longer sticks to the side of the bowl. 3 c or slightly more will be required. Chill for $\frac{1}{2}$ hour.

Place a little of the remaining flour on a board or a clean tabletop and keep the rest handy. Turn dough out onto floured board. Rub a little oil on the hands and form the dough into a rough mound.

To knead. With fingers and palms resting lightly on the dough, gently draw dough towards you. With "heel" of hand, push quickly away. Give the dough a quarter

135

turn and repeat motion, dusting a little flour when necessary, until the dough is satiny smooth with small bubbles forming on the surface. It will spring back when pressed with the finger. This will take from 5 to 10 minutes depending on the efficiency of kneading. (See also photos.)

Place dough in greased bowl and put a little oil on top of dough to prevent a hard crust forming. Cover with a damp cloth and put in a warm place to rise. If you have a warming oven it is ideal for this. Put in, turn on for 1 minute, off for 15, and on for 1 minute again. Leave in warming oven until it has doubled in bulk, and a depression made with the finger remains when it is withdrawn.

Punch dough down and fold sides over. Again leave to rise until it is doubled in bulk. A second rising results in a more tender uniform loaf. Form into 2 large loaves. This is done by dividing in 2 with a knife. Roll out to a 6 inch width and 1 inch thickness. Roll up dough very tightly as for a jelly roll, seal edge by moistening with a little water and turn to bottom. Pull the open ends of the rolled dough underneath and tuck in tightly. This results in a smooth uniform loaf. (See also photos.)

Place in 2 greased 4 inch × 6 inch bread tins, oil top and then let rise until double in bulk under conditions similar to those used before.

Bake in a 375° F oven for 45 to 50 minutes. When done the bottom will sound hollow when tapped with the finger.

Note: Dough should come only halfway up bowls, tins etc., to allow for rising.

Refer to "Sweet Rolls", p. 137, and photos, for instructions on cooking and shaping rolls.

Dough formed into a rough mound ready to knead.

With fingers and palms resting lightly on the dough, gently draw dough towards you.

With "heel" of hand, push quickly away.

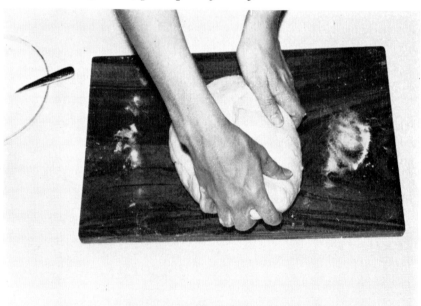

Give the dough a quarter turn and repeat the motion.

Kneaded dough which is satiny smooth with smooth small bubbles forming on the surface.

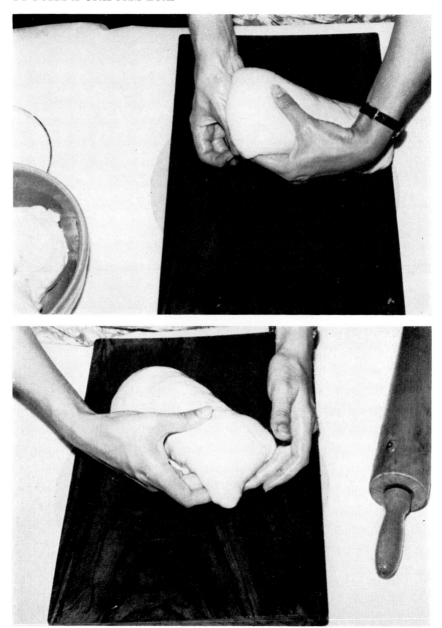

Roll up dough jelly roll fashion and then pull open ends of dough underneath and tuck in tightly.

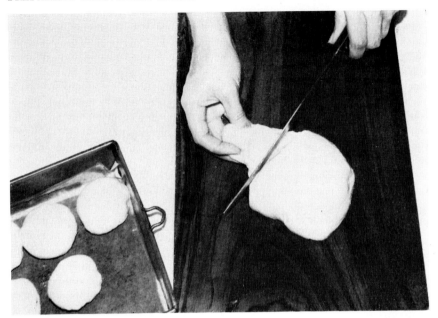

Cut piece of dough required size.

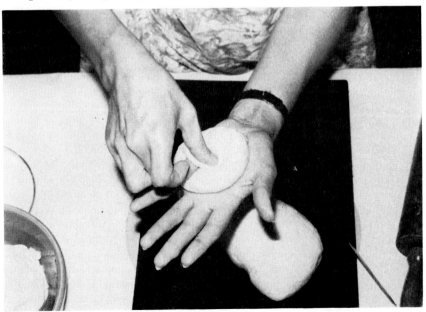

Form into roll by placing dough in palm of hand and pulling up from bottom to top centre with fingers of other hand. Rotate until a smooth round ball is achieved.

Cinnamon rolls

basic dough
sugar
cinnamon
sultanas
butter
Yield:
1½ dozen
Cinnamon rolls

Prepare half basic dough, letting it rise twice.
Prepare a mixture of ¼ c sugar, 1 t cinnamon and ½ c sultanas. Roll out dough until it forms a rectangle, approximately 10 inches × 20 inches. Spread liberally with soft butter, leaving a 1 inch strip along top edge. Cover with sugar mixture, leaving the top edge clear. Roll up, being careful to make it as even and as tight as possible. Seal the top edge to the roll by moistening with a little water. Cut into small rolls 1 inch thick and place cut side up on a greased tray. Let it rise until double in bulk.
Bake in a 400° F oven for 15 minutes or until golden and risen.
Refer to Sweet Rolls, below, for instructions on baking and shaping rolls.

Sweet rolls

yeast
water
milk
butter
sugar
salt
eggs
flour
oil
Yield:
2 dozen rolls

Refer to Basic White Bread for general instructions.
Place 2 T dried yeast and ¼ c lukewarm water in a warm bowl. Leave for 10 minutes.
Scald 1 c milk, add ⅓ c butter, ½ c sugar and 1 t salt. Let cool until lukewarm. Beat into yeast mixture. Add 2 eggs and 2 c sifted flour. Beat for 5 minutes with electric beaters or 10 minutes by hand with wooden spoon. Cover and let rise for 40 minutes or until double in bulk. Add a further 3–3½ c sifted flour or enough to make the dough just firm enough to handle. Chill for ½ hour. Knead, adding a little more flour if necessary, until dough is satiny smooth with small air bubbles on the surface.
Place dough in greased bowl, cover and let rise until double in bulk. Punch down. Form dough into small individual rolls by

137

placing dough in the palm of the hand and pulling up from bottom to top centre with fingers of other hand. Rotate until a smooth round ball is achieved. (See also photos.) Place on greased baking sheet. Lightly oil and let rise until double in bulk. Bake 12 to 15 minutes at 400°–425° F.

Hot cross buns

sweet roll dough
mixed spice
sultanas
currants
mixed peel
flour
water
sugar
milk
Yield:
  2 dozen rolls

Follow recipe for Sweet Rolls, but add 1 T mixed spice with salt. Add $\frac{1}{2}$ c sultanas, $\frac{1}{4}$ c currants and 2 T mixed peel with last 3–$3\frac{1}{2}$ c flour.
After forming into rolls, beat $\frac{1}{4}$ c flour with sufficient water to make a thick batter. Pipe dough on tops of buns to form a cross. This will not brown while baking. Whilst baking, brush a couple of times with a mixture of 1 T sugar and 2 T milk. This will result in a lovely brown glaze.

Apple yeast cake

sweet roll dough
butter
apple
sugar
cinnamon
currants or
  sultanas
Serves: 8

Follow recipe for Sweet Roll Dough. After it has been kneaded and left to rise until double in bulk, punch down and divide into equal parts or prepare half of dough. Line and grease 1 layer cake tin. Spread $\frac{1}{2}$ of dough evenly into tin. Brush with 1 T melted butter.
Peel, core and slice 3 cooking apples. Press into dough to form a circle, sharp edge down. Sprinkle with $\frac{1}{4}$ c sugar mixed with $\frac{1}{2}$ t powdered cinnamon and 2 T currants or sultanas.
Cover and let rise until double in bulk. Bake at 350° F for 30 minutes or until done. Slice and serve hot with butter for morning coffee. This reheats very well if it is desirable to prepare it ahead of time.

138

Use rest of dough as required or make double quantity of cake.
Very good with tea or morning coffee.

Scones

Basic plain scones

flour
baking powder
salt
margarine
milk
Yield: 1½ dozen

Measure and sift 2 c flour, 3 t baking powder, and 1 t salt in a bowl.
Cut 6 level T margarine (3 oz or 75 g) into flour mixture as finely as possible using 2 knives. Continue working in the margarine by rubbing it gently through the hands until a coarse meal like consistency is reached.
Measure ⅔ c milk. Slowly add this to the mixture whilst stirring with a fork. Add milk only to the dry areas, reserving the last 2 T.
Check the consistency before adding more. It should be a soft, pliable and non sticky dough. Slowly add sufficient of the remaining milk to achieve this consistency.
Form into a ball, place on a slightly floured board and knead half a dozen times.
Roll out scones to ½ inch thickness. Cut into rounds, using a 2-inch biscuit cutter.
Fit leftover pieces together as rolling will toughen the mixture. Place on an ungreased baking sheet and bake in a hot (425° F) oven for 12 to 14 minutes.
They will be done when they are a light golden brown with raised layered sides.
Remove from oven and serve at once with butter or whipped cream and jam. Delicious for afternoon teas.
Variations:
Coconut scones. Substitute coconut cream for milk in Plain Scones. These are slightly richer with a delicate coconut flavour which is savoury rather than sweet.

Cheese scones. Add ½ c finely grated Cheddar cheese to the flour mixture before adding the milk in Plain Scones. These scones have a delicate cheesey flavour.

Herb scones. Add 1 t mixed herbs and ¼ t dry mustard to flour mixture before the addition of the milk in Plain Scones. Ideal with cold meat salad.

Duruka pinwheels

cheese scone dough
duruka
water
Yield:
  3 dozen
  pinwheels

Prepare Cheese Scone dough. Parboil (5 minutes) 8 sticks duruka. Drain well and cool.

Roll scone mixture out to ¼ inch thickness. Cut into strips 5 inches wide. Lay 2–3 duruka on dough and roll up jelly roll fashion. Moisten, join with water to seal. Cut into ¾ inch slices. Place on ungreased baking sheet, cut side up.

Bake 425° F for 12 to 15 minutes. They will be raised and slightly brown when done. Serve plain or cut in half and spread with butter. Excellent for afternoon tea or as a savoury for a party.

Sweet pumpkin scones

margarine
caster sugar
water
pumpkin
baking powder
flour
cornflour
salt
Yield: 16 scones

Cream 2 T margarine with ½ c caster sugar. Add 1 T hot water and beat well. Beat in ¾ c cold, cooked and sieved pumpkin. Sift 2½ t baking powder, 1½ c flour, 2 T corn-flour and ½ t salt together. Fold into pumpkin mixture.

Turn out onto floured board. Knead ½ dozen times. Pat out to ¾ inch thickness. Cut into rounds using a 2 inch biscuit cutter. Place on greased baking sheet.

Bake in 425° F oven for 12 to 15 minutes. When risen and golden, remove and place on wire rack to cool.

Serve plain with butter or jelly.

Perfect for afternoon or morning tea.

140

Sweet fruit scones

flour
salt
baking powder
margarine
sugar
dried mixed fruit,
(sultanas,raisins,
or dates)
egg
milk

Yield: 20 scones

Yield: 2 dozen

Sift 2 c flour, $\frac{1}{2}$ t salt and 3 t baking powder together. Work $\frac{1}{4}$ c margarine into mixture using two knives and then hands as directed in Basic Plain Scones. Mix in $\frac{1}{4}$ c sugar and $\frac{3}{4}$ c dried mixed fruit (sultanas, raisins or dates).

Beat 1 egg with $\frac{1}{2}$ c milk. Slowly add to flour mixture until no dry areas are left and a soft, non-sticky dough is achieved; it may not be necessary to use all the liquid. Turn out onto floured board. Knead $\frac{1}{2}$ dozen times. Pat or roll dough out until it is $\frac{3}{4}$ inch thick. Cut into rounds using a floured 2 inch biscuit cutter. Place on greased baking sheet. Bake in 425° F oven for 12 to 15 minutes or until risen and golden brown.
Place on wire rack to cool.

Variation:
Sweet Coconut Scones. Prepare Sweet Fruit Scones but reduce milk to $\frac{1}{3}$ c. Beat 1 c freshly grated coconut into egg and milk before adding to dry ingredients.
Bake as directed for Sweet Fruit Scones. Just a little bit special.

Banana scones

flour
salt
baking powder
caster sugar
butter
banana
egg
milk

Yield: 1$\frac{1}{2}$ dozen scones

Sift 2 c flour, $\frac{1}{2}$ t salt, 3 t baking powder and $\frac{1}{4}$ c caster sugar together. Melt 2 T butter. Mash sufficient banana to yield $\frac{1}{2}$ cup. Beat banana, butter, 1 egg and 2 T milk together.
Make a hollow in flour mixture. Pour liquid in and mix with a fork just until there are no areas of flour left.
Drop onto a greased biscuit sheet, using 2 spoons. Bake in 400° F oven for 15 minutes or until golden and risen.
Delicious plain or with butter and so quick to make.

141

Variations:
Kumala Scones (sweet potato). **Prepare** Banana Scones adding 1 t powdered cinnamon and ½ t grated nutmeg to dry ingredients. Substitute ½ c cooked mashed kumala for banana. Increase milk to ½ c plus 2 T. Bake as directed for Banana Scones.

Yield: 1½ dozen scones

Breadfruit Scones. Prepare Banana Scones, folding ½ c sultanas into dry ingredients, substituting ½ c cooked mashed breadfruit for banana. Increase milk to ½ c plus 2 T. Bake as directed for banana scones.
A good way of using leftover breadfruit.

Pancakes

Basic pancakes (crêpes)

flour
sugar
salt
eggs
butter
milk
Yield:
  1 dozen large
  or 2 dozen
  small pancakes

Sift 1 c flour, 1 T sugar and ⅛ t salt together. Beat 3 eggs into flour mixture, one at a time; beating well after each addition. Melt 2 T butter, blend with 1½ c milk. Slowly beat into flour mixture. Leave to stand for 2 hours.
Lightly butter very hot 10 inch fry pan for large pancakes or 5 to 6 inch pan for smaller ones. Pour ¼ c batter into large pan or about 2 T into small. Tilt pan around until batter is evenly distributed and ceases to run. When it is dry on top with fine bubbles, flip it over with the aid of a spatula. Cook for ½ minute more.
Remove to wire rack and keep warm. Stack succeeding pancakes.
Omit sugar for savoury pancakes.
Serve as a luncheon dish or as dessert with coffee in one of the following ways:

SAVOURY PANCAKES

Chilli crab pancakes
basic pancakes

Prepare Pancakes. Fill and roll using ½

142

chilli crab
lemon juice
parsley
Serves: 4

quantity of hot Chilli Crab (p. 26). Sprinkle with lemon juice and finely chopped parsley.

Mushroom and kidney pancakes
basic pancakes
butter
mushroom and
  kidney filling
milk
spring onions
Serves: 4

Prepare Pancakes and lightly smear with butter. Roll and place in serving dish. Pour over hot Mushroom and Kidney Filling (p. 27) which has been slightly thinned with 2 to 4 T milk.
Garnish with chopped spring onions.

Fish and stuffed olives pancakes
basic pancakes
fish and stuffed
  olive filling
cheese
Serves: 4

Prepare Pancakes. Fill and roll using $\frac{1}{2}$ quantity of hot Fish and Stuffed Olive Filling (p. 26). Place in serving dish and sprinkle with $\frac{1}{2}$ c grated cheese. Place in hot oven or under griller for a couple of minutes to melt cheese before serving.

Sockeye salmon and spring onion pancakes
basic pancakes
butter
sockeye salmon and
  spring onion
  filling
milk
Serves: 4

Prepare Pancakes and lightly smear with butter. Roll and place in serving dish. Pour over hot Sockeye Salmon and Spring Onion Filling (p. 26) which has been thinned with 2 to 4 T milk.
Variation: Substitute tuna for salmon.

Pacific Island pancakes
basic pancakes
butter
Pacific island filling
prawns
cucumber
milk
Serves: 4

Prepare Pancakes and lightly smear with butter. Roll and place in serving dish. Pour over hot Pacific Island Filling (p. 28) which has been prepared with cooked prawns and raw cucumber. Thin to desired consistency with 2 to 4 T milk.

143

Cheesey corned silverside pancakes

basic white sauce
corned silverside
Cheddar cheese
basic pancakes
Serves: 4

Prepare 1 c Basic White Sauce (p. 26). Add ½ c finely chopped cooked corned silverside and ⅓ c grated Cheddar cheese. Prepare Pancakes. Fill with hot sauce and roll up. Place in serving dish. Sprinkle with grated cheese and place under griller for a couple of minutes to melt cheese before serving.

DESSERT PANCAKES
Excellent in the evening with coffee.

Lemon pancakes

basic pancakes
butter
caster sugar
lemon juice
Serves: 6

Prepare Pancakes. Smear with butter and roll up.
Sprinkle with caster sugar and lemon juice.

Coconut cream pancakes with chocolate

basic pancakes
whipped cream
freshly grated
  coconut
dark chocolate
Serves: 6

Prepare Pancakes and keep hot. Mix 1 c whipped cream with 1 c freshly grated coconut. Spread liberally on pancakes and roll up. Melt a 3 oz bar of dark chocolate over low heat. Dribble over pancakes and serve immediately.

Banana sour cream pancakes

basic pancakes
banana
reduced cream
lemon juice
caster sugar
Serves: 6

Prepare Pancakes and keep hot. Mix ½ c mashed banana with ½ c reduced cream, 1 T lemon juice and 1 T caster sugar. Spread liberally on pancakes, roll up and sprinkle with a little caster sugar.

Pastry

Detailed basic short crust pastry
(Suitable for Tropical Climate)

flour
salt

Measure 2 c flour and 1 t salt. Sift into a chilled mixing bowl. Measure ½ c and 2 T

144

margarine
Yield: sufficient
for 9 inch
2 crusted pie

margarine. Have the margarine firm, but not hard.

Take 2 table knives and place one in each hand. Using a scissorlike motion, cut through the fat until pieces the size of marbles are achieved. Now rub pastry through your hands gently, being careful not to squeeze the fat in your fingers. It is the motion of the fat and the flour on itself rather than the pressure of your hands, that is needed. Continue until the particles of fat are the size of small dried peas.

Measure $\frac{1}{4}$ c ice cold water. This is just a guide as a little more or less may be required. Add the water slowly to the pastry mixture while stirring with a fork.

Only add water to dry areas. This is a safeguard against adding too much.

When there are no longer dry areas and the pastry is lumping together, form into a smooth ball with your hands. The dough should be soft and pliable but not sticky.

Rolling out pastry for a 9-inch pie

Prepare $\frac{1}{2}$ of Basic Short Crust Pastry and smooth it into a pancake-like shape with the hands. Sprinkle flour on the rolling surface and on the rolling pin or round bottle. Starting at the centre, roll out the pastry, lifting the rolling pin as the edge is approached. This is done in order to keep the pastry the same thickness throughout. Roll out equally in all directions, striving to achieve as perfect a circle as possible. A heavy hand with pastry toughens it; surprisingly little pressure is needed to roll it out.

When it is $\frac{1}{8}$ inch thick and about 2 inches larger than the outside rim of the pie plate, fold it in half. Putting both hands underneath to support the pastry and prevent

K

stretching, transfer to the pie plate and unfold.
Gently ease it down to fit the bottom and sides, being careful again not to stretch it. Trim edge to within an inch of outside rim. Turn this excess pastry under and smooth the edges even with the outside rim. The edge may be finished by simply pressing with a fork or a more attractive way is as follows: with the thumb of left hand, press in from the outside. At the same time, using the thumb and first finger of your right hand, press back from the inside. A raised scalloped edge is achieved when this is repeated evenly all the way round.

Baked pastry shell

Using a fork, prick the sides and bottom of the shell thoroughly to prevent large bubbles from forming during baking, or bake blind by filling with dried beans placed on a circle of greaseproof paper. Place in 425° F oven and bake for about 10 minutes. Watch closely so that it doesn't burn. Cool and add any cold filling desired.

Two-crusted pie

Prepare Basic Short Crust Pastry. Using $\frac{1}{2}$ of pastry prepare bottom crust as previously directed but trim pastry even with rim and do not prick. Fill with desired filling. Roll out second piece of pastry until it is about 2 inches wider than pie plate. Fold in half and cut a design through the pastry; this will allow steam to escape.
Moisten the rim of the bottom crust with water. Place pastry on top and unfold. Trim to within $\frac{3}{4}$ inch of pie plate. Gently fold the top crust under the bottom.
Finish the edge as previously directed for a 1 crust pie.
Bake as directed in individual pie recipes.

Sweet pastry

flour
salt
sugar
margarine or lard
egg
milk
Yield: sufficient
for 9 inch
2-crusted pie

Sift together 2 c flour, ½ t salt and 2 T sugar. Cut in 4 oz margarine or lard, using the method given for Basic Short Crust Pastry.
Beat together 1 egg and sufficient milk to yield ¾ c. Stir this into dry areas until a firm pliable ball of pastry is formed.
Proceed as directed for Short Crust Pastry. Use as desired for any sweet pie.

Sweet crumb pastry

sweet plain biscuits
butter
Yield: shell for 1
8 inch pie dish
or springform
pan

Prepare by crushing with rolling pin 1 c sweet plain biscuit crumbs. Melt 2 T butter. Stir into biscuits. Press into dish or pan, using bottom and sides of a glass. Refrigerate for ½ hour before using, to allow it to partially set.

Breadfruit pastry

breadfruit
margarine
salt
Yield: 8 inch pie
shell

Prepare 1 c cooked sieved breadfruit. Place in a mixing bowl and blend in 1 T margarine and ½ t salt.
Turn out on to floured board and knead two or three times. Roll out into desired shape.
Bake as for Basic Short Crust Pastry.
Makes an excellent type of vol-au-vent case and shell for savoury pies.

Cheese straws

basic short crust
pastry
egg
Cheddar cheese
caraway or
sesame seeds
Yield: 2 dozen

Prepare Short Crust Pastry. Roll out into a ¼ inch thick rectangle. Brush with beaten egg. Sprinkle with ½ c grated Cheddar cheese and 1 T caraway or sesame seeds. Gently pat cheese to ensure that it sticks to the pastry. Cut into strips ¼ inch wide and 6 inches long. Twist like a corkscrew. Place on greased biscuit sheet 1 inch apart. Bake in 400° F oven for 10 to 12 minutes or until crisp and slightly brown. Cool on rack

147

and then store in airtight container. These may be reheated in a slow oven for 10 minutes before serving. They also freeze and reheat well.

A perfect savoury with before dinner drinks.

Using Sharps

Detailed preparation of roti

sharps (ata)
salt
water
ghee
Yield: 1½ dozen

Allow
1–2 per woman
2–3 per man

Sift 3½ c sharps (ata—coarse wheat flour) and ¼ t salt into a large, flat bottom, shallow bowl. Using a fork, stir in 1¼ to 1½ c boiling water. This amount will vary depending on the sharps. Add water slowly, stirring well after each addition until the mixture begins to stick together. You will still have some dry sharps left at this point.

Knead in bowl until rest of sharps has been incorporated and a smooth ball has been formed. Continue to add and knead in a little more sharps until the dough is pliable and non sticky.

Knead 1 T ghee into dough. At this stage the knuckles rather than the palms of the hands are more helpful. Continue kneading until a soft, pliable non sticky dough is again achieved.

Pinch off 2 oz (50 g) piece of dough. Roll in hands to form smooth round ball. Dip in little sharps and then form a round thick disc by working with hands. Dip again in sharps. Roll out to ⅛ inch thickness. Brush centre section with ghee. Fold bottom up, top down and sides in (as in puff pastry). Roll out to form a square or round from 6 to 8 inches in diameter (depending on weight of original ball of dough).

Cook on very hot roti iron or in electric fry pan which has been lightly smeared with ghee.

148

Cook for 10–15 seconds on one side (until beginning to brown). Flip over using metal spatula. Brown again while brushing top with ghee. Turn to original side, brush with ghee and cook for a moment longer. (While roti is being cooked in the pan and brushed with ghee, do quarter turns with fingers to prevent burning. Roti should be tender and flat whilst the colour will be golden with dark brown spots.)
Place on absorbent paper in dish to keep warm. Serve with curries.

Puri

sharps (ata)
salt
water
ghee
Yield: 2 dozen

Allow
2–3 per woman
3–4 per man

Prepare dough using 1 lb ($\frac{1}{2}$ kg) sharps (ata) as directed in Preparation of Roti. Instead of forming balls of dough by pinching off pieces, roll dough out until it is about $\frac{3}{8}$ inch thick. Cut into rounds with a 2 inch biscuit cutter (this ensures ease and uniformity in final rolling).
Heat a good inch of ghee in fry pan until very hot. Dip puris in a little sharps and then roll out until $\frac{1}{8}$ inch thick. Immerse in hot fat, dipping with fork to cover. Cook for about 30 seconds (will begin to puff), turn and cook for about 30 seconds more, (will be very puffed).
Place on absorbent paper in casserole dish. Press succeeding ones down firmly on top. Keep hot until ready to serve.
Should be tender, flaky and slightly crisper than rotis. They are a golden colour with no dark spots. Puris are richer than rotis since they are immersed in fat.
Serve with curries.
Note: a substitute for sharps would be a coarsely ground white or wholemeal flour.

149

Cakes and Biscuits

Lolo coconut cake

eggs
sugar
vanilla essence
flour
cornflour
baking powder
salt
thick coconut cream
coconut
butter
brown sugar
Yield: one 8-inch
 square cake plus
 topping

Beat 2 eggs. Gradually add 1 c sugar and continue beating until mixture is thick and light. Add 1 t vanilla.
Sift 1 c minus 1 T flour, 1 T cornflour, 1 t baking powder and ¼ t salt together. Slowly add to egg mixture, mixing well after each addition. Prepare ½ c plus 1 T very thick coconut cream. Heat to boiling point (do not allow to boil). Fold into mixture.
Bake in greased and floured 8 inch square tin in 350° F oven for 40 to 50 minutes. It will spring back when pressed with the finger and be golden brown when done.
Prepare topping of 1 c freshly grated coconut, 3 T melted butter and 5 T brown sugar. Spread evenly over hot cake and place under griller for 3 to 4 minutes or until brown. This must be watched closely so it does not burn.
Leave in tin to cool.

Chocolate cake

water
cocoa
soda bicarbonate
butter
sugar
eggs
vanilla
vinegar
milk
flour
cornflour
salt
Yield: one 8-inch
 layer cake

Heat ½ c water with ½ c cocoa and 1½ t soda bicarbonate over low heat, stirring until a smooth paste has been formed. Remove from heat and allow to cool.
Beat ⅔ c butter with 1¾ c sugar until light and fluffy. Beat in 2 eggs and 1 t vanilla.
Add 2 t vinegar to 1 c milk. Stir and allow to stand for 5 minutes.
Sift 2 c flour with ½ c cornflour and ½ t salt. Beat cooled chocolate into butter mixture and then alternately add soured milk and dry ingredients beating well after each addition.
Pour into two 8-inch round cake tins which have been lined, greased and floured.
Bake at 350° F oven for 30 to 40 minutes.

150

When done remove from oven and leave in tins for 5 minutes before turning out onto cake racks. Ice with the following rum flavoured chocolate frosting.

Chocolate rum frosting

cocoa
icing sugar
egg
butter
milk
rum or vanilla
Yield: sufficient
   to ice an 8-inch
   layer cake

Sift $\frac{1}{2}$ c cocoa with 2 c icing sugar. Thoroughly blend 1 egg, and $\frac{1}{3}$ c butter. Add sugar mixture and $\frac{1}{4}$ c milk alternately, beating well after each addition. Flavour with 1 t rum or $\frac{1}{2}$ t vanilla.

Banana tea bread

flour
baking powder
soda
salt
caster sugar
eggs
bananas
butter
Yield: one
   $5\frac{1}{2} \times 9\frac{1}{2}$ inch
   loaf tin or two
   4 × 6 inch tins

Sift together $3\frac{1}{2}$ c flour, 3 t baking powder, $\frac{1}{2}$ t soda, 1 t salt and $1\frac{1}{3}$ c sugar. Mix together 4 eggs, 2 c well mashed bananas and $\frac{1}{2}$ c melted butter. Stir liquid quickly and lightly into dry ingredients just until whole mixture is moistened. Spoon mixture into a large $9\frac{1}{2} \times 5\frac{1}{2}$ inch loaf tin or 2 small 4 × 6 inch pans which have been greased. Bake in moderate (350° F) oven for 50 to 60 minutes for the small tins and 70 to 80 minutes for the large one. It will have risen, be golden brown with cracks across the top when done. Allow to cool in pan before removing. This is excellent for freezing. Serve with butter or just plain as desired. *Variation:* Add $\frac{1}{2}$ c dried mixed fruit.

Coconut chocolate chip biscuits

butter
sugar
eggs

Beat $\frac{2}{3}$ c butter and $1\frac{1}{2}$ c sugar together until light and fluffy. Add 2 eggs, 2 t vanilla and beat well.

151

vanilla
flour
soda
salt
chocolate chips
desiccated coconut
Yield: 4½ dozen

Sift 2 c flour, 1 t soda and 1 t salt together Fold into egg butter mixture. Stir in 1, 5½ oz package chocolate chips and 1 c desiccated or fresh dried coconut. Drop onto greased biscuit sheets using 2 teaspoons. Leave plenty of room between these biscuits as they spread.
Bake in 375° F oven for 10 to 12 minutes. When done, they will be slightly brown and flat. Remove from oven, allow to cool for a couple of minutes before transferring to a biscuit rack.
Note: Place freshly grated coconut in a shallow pan in 200–250° F oven. Stir occasionally and bake until dry and crumbly to the touch.

Rolled oat fruit biscuits

butter
golden syrup
egg
milk
flour
baking powder
salt
rolled oats
dried mixed fruit
Yield: 40 biscuits

Combine ½ c soft butter with ½ c golden syrup. Beat in 1 egg and 2 T milk.
Sift 1⅓ c flour, 2 t baking powder and ½ t salt together. Blend with 1⅓ c rolled oats and ½ c mixed fruit. Fold into syrup mixture.
Drop rounded teaspoonsful on to greased biscuit sheets. Bake in 375° F oven 10 to 12 minutes. They will be golden brown, raised and firm when done. Remove from tray immediately.
These non-sweet nutritious biscuits are perfect to send along as part of a school lunch.

Never fail meringues

egg whites
caster sugar
lemon juice or
    vinegar
vanilla
baking powder

Separate 3 eggs. Mix the egg whites with 2 c caster sugar and 2 t lemon juice or vinegar. Leave for 10 minutes. Add 2 T boiling water. Place bowl over hot water and beat until mixture is stiff enough to hold its shape. Fold in 1 t vanilla and 2 t baking

152

boiling water
Yield: 4 dozen

powder. Put teaspoonsful of mixture on oiled greaseproof paper or make one large Pavlova Cake (see below). Bake at 250° F until firm and crisp. Turn off oven and leave to dry out.

To make a Pavlova cake

Oil a sheet of greaseproof paper and put on oven tray. Make a circle of meringue mixture 6–8 inches in diameter and about ¾ inch deep. Form a raised edge round the circle by piping or spooning on extra meringue. Alternatively, make a circular pile of meringue on paper and spread the mixture to the edge leaving a hollow in the centre. Bake at 200–250° F till firm and dry. The cake should be loose on the paper.

Fill the centre with one of the following:

1. Brandied pawpaw whip, p. 128.
2. Whipped cream flavoured with Tia Maria liqueur. To 2 c cream add 2 T Tia Maria spread over Pavlova Cake and then sprinkle with chocolate "bits" or grated dark chocolate.
3. Whipped cream flavoured with passion fruit and sugar. To 2 c cream add ⅔ c passion fruit pulp and ¼ c–½ c sugar.
4. Lime cream filling.

Lime cream filling

egg yolks
lime or lemon juice
grated lime skin
sugar
gelatin
water
cream
green colour

Beat 2 yolks with ½ c sugar. Add 1 t grated rind and ¼ c lemon or lime juice. Cook in a double boiler till the mixture thickens. Soften 1 t gelatin in 2 t water. Stir into hot mixture. Cool.
Fold in 1 c cream which has been whipped. Colour pale green.
Variations: Peppermint. Substitute ⅓ Crème de Menthe for sugar and lemon juice and garnish with a sprig of mint.

Baba rhum cakes

water
yeast
flour

Place ½ c lukewarm water in a mixing bowl. Sprinkle 1 T dried yeast over it. Let stand for 5 to 10 minutes. Beat in ½ c flour and

153

eggs
sugar
salt
butter
rum
Yield: 24 small
cakes

then 4 eggs, one at a time, beating well after each addition. Sift $\frac{1}{4}$ c sugar, $\frac{1}{8}$ t salt and 1 c flour together. Beat into dough. Cover and let rise until light, about 40 to 60 minutes. Beat in $\frac{1}{2}$ c soft butter, a little at a time. Butter 24 pattie tins and fill $\frac{2}{3}$ full with batter. Cover and let stand for 10 to 15 minutes. Bake in hot 375°–400° F oven until risen and brown. Remove from tins and allow to cool on rack.

Prepare rum sauce by boiling 1 c sugar with 1 c water for 10 minutes. Add $\frac{1}{4}$ c rum. Dip cooled cakes in sauce.

Serve plain with coffee or as a dessert with cream.

Variation:

Peach Baba Rhum. Prepare and dip baba cakes as directed. Just before serving, cut the bottom off well drained peach halves. Place peach halves in a dish with inside facing up. Cut a slit in top of baba cake and insert slice cut from base of peach. Place baba cake in hollow of peach in dish and top with whipped cream. Pour a little rum syrup over top and serve.

Lemon mellow

eggs
sweetened condensed
   milk
lemon juice
lemon rind
sponge layer
caster sugar
Serves: 6

Separate 2 eggs. Beat egg yolks with 8 oz sweetened condensed milk, $\frac{1}{2}$ c lemon juice and grated rind of 1 lemon. Evenly spread over a prepared sponge layer.

Beat egg whites until stiff, but not dry. Gradually beat in $\frac{1}{2}$ c caster sugar. Spread over filling, being careful to seal cake. Bake in a slow (300° F) oven for 15 to 20 minutes till meringue is firm.

An impressive dessert when something a little bit special is required at the last moment.

154

Vegetables

In tropical climates many varieties of green leafy vegetables, beans and fruits are to be found in the markets and gardens. Nowadays horticultural research has also provided tropical countries with strains of tomatoes, lettuce and other temperate vegetables, which will thrive in hot wet climates.

Many of the tropical vegetables have a good flavour and texture but as with all foods, the right methods of preparation and cooking must be used.

All the dark green leafy spinach type vegetables like taro leaves, kang kong, bele and the red and yellow fruits like pumpkin and sweet peppers, have a high vitamin value. Beans and gourd type fruits like cucumber and Chinese marrow have the same food values as similar varieties grown in temperate climates.

In the vegetable chart we have described the best ways of preparing and cooking some of the more common tropical vegetables.

Vegetable Chart

Variety	Selection	Storage	Preparation and Uses
BEANS LONG BEANS or COW PEAS	Choose young green beans	Keep in plastic bag in refrigerator or in covered container in cool place	Cut diagonally in thin slices with very sharp knife or razor blade. Cook in boiling salted water for 5 minutes. Season with a little butter and pepper. For variation, flavour with a little fresh chopped basil. Blanch a few almonds, cut in fine slices, sauté in butter until golden and toss with beans. Use cold in salads and in vegetables curries. Prepare Hot Beans (p. 167). Prepare Long Bean Salad (p. 57).
FRILLY WINGED BEANS	Choose small young beans.	Keep in plastic bag in refrigerator or in covered container in cool place.	Trim off ends and part of the frilly edge. Slice diagonally and treat similarly to long beans.
SWORD BEANS	Choose small immature beans. Mature beans are tough.	Keep in plastic bag in refrigerator or in covered container in cool place.	Remove strings. Cut diagonally and put into boiling salted water. Cook for 7 to 10 minutes. Treat similarly to long beans, using variations as desired.
CHOKO (Chocho, Chayote Cristophene)	Choose clean white or pale green fruit. There should be no sign of the fruit sprouting at the end. This indicates an old stringy fruit.	On wire racks, keeps several days.	Peel under running water (prevent staining), cut in halves, quarters or dice. Use in curries or stews. Boil in salted water until tender and serve with white sauce, cheese or tomato flavoured sauce. Use cold diced choko in salads. Toss in French Dressing (p. 50), and garnish with chives.

| DURUKA | Choose stems with tightly furled buds. | Stand bundles upright in cool place. Keeps 24 hours. This vegetable freezes well. | Break off section containing the duruka bud carefully. Remove the leaves and discard. Place durukas in casserole and cover with seasoned milk or coconut cream. Bake until tender. Steam durukas, drain well. Serve with coconut cream or cheese sauce. Prepare Duruka Crayfish (p. 86). Use cold cooked duruka in salads, marinated in French Dressing (p. 50), or Miti (p. 181). Prepare Duruka Pinwheels (p. 140). Do not remove all leaves from flower. Bake durukas in oven until soft. Remove and discard leaves and use as above or serve hot with butter, salt and pepper. Cooking the leaves preserves flavour. |
| EGGPLANT (Aubergine, Baigan, Baigani) | Fruit should be firm, fully developed but not hard at the ends. Over ripe eggplant is full of seeds. Colour is not an indication of ripeness as varieties vary from dark purple to white. | On wire racks or covered in refrigerator. Keeps several days. | Peel fruit, slice or cube and use as base for soup as in Eggplant Soup (p. 45), as sauce in Lamb with Eggplant Sauce (p. 92), as an appetiser in Eggplant Hors d'Oeuvres (p. 38), or as a spread in Eggplant Caviar (p. 33). Use in curries and casseroles as in Eggplant Escalope (p. 95) and Eggplant and Olives (p. 167). Prepare Sweet and Sour Eggplant Salad (p. 56). Cut into slices, dip in milk and flour or batter and fry. Leave skin on, scoop out centre and stuff with meat or vegetables as in Stuffed Eggplant (p. 168). Prepare Steak Baigan (p. 99). |

Variety	Selection	Storage	Preparation and Uses
PAWPAW GREEN or HALF RIPE PAPAYA	Fruit must be well formed and firm.	On rack.	Peel and use in the same way as gourds. Half ripe pawpaw may be stuffed with meat mixture as in Stuffed Eggplant (p. 168). Use green pawpaw to tenderize tough meat. Add to stew or casseroles. Use in pickles as in Fresh Green Pawpaw Pickle (p. 183).
WHITE RADISH	Young crisp roots. Older roots become very hot.	In refrigerator or cool place. Keeps several days.	Peel and use in soups, stews. Grate or slice thinly and use raw in salads. Prepare Banana Radish Dressing (p. 51). Use in Chinese vegetable dishes. Use in pickles as in Oriental Vegetable Pickle (p. 182).
GOURDS— VARIETIES: CHINESE MARROW, ROUND, BOTTLE, LONG GOURDS, SNAKE BEAN, LAUKI, LUFFA, TAROI	Fruit should be young and firm; older fruit contains too many seeds and flesh is spongy.	On racks. Keep several days.	Peel or scrape. Cut into slices or dice. Steam boil in salted water. Drain well. Serve with White Sauce (p. 26) or with flavoured sauce of cheese or tomato. Use in curries, stews and soup as in Tropical Vegetable (p. 46). Choose medium sized fruit. Cut off top, scoop out centre and stuff with meat, vegetables and rice mixtures. Use in Eggplant and Olives (p. 167).
KOHLRABI	Roots must be young otherwise the flesh is tough and fibrous.	On rack or in refrigerator.	Remove tops. If very young, these may be used as a green vegetable. Peel roots and slice or dice. Steam or boil in salted water and serve with White Sauce (p. 26) or cheese sauce. Use in soups, curries and stews. Slice thinly and use raw in salads.

OKRA (Bhindi)	Pods should be young and soft. About 2 to 3 inches long.	Place in plastic bags and store in refrigerator or in covered container in cool place.	Remove stems. Put whole pods in boiling salted water, drain and serve with butter. Cook, cool and serve as salad with French Dressing (p. 50). Slice and combine with other vegetables in Okra Gumbo (p. 168). Slice, dip in batter and fry in hot oil. Use as a base for curry.

GREEN LEAFY VEGETABLES

CREEPING SPINACH	Young stems with large tender leaves.	Wash and store in plastic bags in refrigerator or place in covered container in cool place.	Remove leaves from stems and leave whole. Cook leaves in a small quantity of boiling salted water for 3 to 4 minutes. Drain, season with butter or coconut cream.
INDIAN SPINACH (Bhagi) WATER SPINACH (Water kumala, Kang Kong)	Young stems with large tender leaves.	Wash and store in plastic bags in refrigerator or place in covered container in cool place.	As given in Creeping Spinach or wash leaves and then cook in saucepan with a little butter, stirring frequently until soft. Prepare Cream of Bhagi Soup (p. 44).
BELE	Pick young top leaves.	Wash and store in plastic bags in refrigerator or place in covered container in cool place.	Cook whole leaves in boiling water for 2 minutes, turn and cook for another 2 minutes. Serve with butter or coconut cream.
WATERCRESS	Young stems with large leaves.	Wash and store in plastic bags in refrigerator or place in covered container in cool place.	Wash well in several waters. Use as a salad. Cook in chicken stock and use as a base for cream soup.

L

161

Variety	Selection	Storage	Preparation and Uses
CHINESE CABBAGE	Green tender leaves and firm white stalks.	Wash and store in plastic bags in refrigerator or place in covered container in cool place.	Young cabbages may be used as salad greens as in Chinese Cabbage and Carrot (p. 58). Remove leaf from stalk. Cut leaves and stalks into diagonal strips. Boil stalks 3 to 4 minutes in salted water. Add leaves and boil for a further 2 to 3 minutes. Drain and season with butter. Sauté washed leaves in a little butter or oil in pan. Add a little water, cover and steam until tender. Season with salt. Sauté a little onion and garlic in oil or butter. Add prepared cabbage and sauté 2 to 3 minutes. Add a little water and cook until tender. Use in soups like Beef and Chinese Cabbage (p. 43).
SWEET POTATO TOPS PUMPKIN TOPS	Young shoots with crisp stems and young leaves.	Wash and store in plastic bags in refrigerator or place in covered container in cool place.	Break young crisp stems into 1 inch pieces or leave whole. Remove larger leaves. Cook in boiling salted water for 2–5 minutes. Serve with butter. Prepare as above and cook in boiling coconut cream.

	Description	Storage	Preparation
OTA FERN	Young shoots with tightly curled frond.	Cut off the lower part of the stem which is hard and fibrous. Store crisp stalks in plastic bags in refrigerator or in a covered container in a cool place.	Cut stems into even lengths (about 3–4 inches). Test the crispness of the stem by snapping. With the tip of a sharp knife, strip each stem into quarters. Arrange lengthwise and tie in a bundle. Cook in boiling salted water for 5 minutes. Drain and serve with butter and a slice of lemon or with Miti (p. 181). Prepare stems same way, but do not tie. Put into boiling salted water, boil for 1 minute. Turn over and boil for 1 minute more. Remove, drain well, serve as above or cold with French Dressing (p. 50). Make Kora Banana Ota (p. 59).
ROU ROU (Taro leaves)	Young leaves with green stems. Old leaves and those of certain purple stemmed varieties, contain oxalate crystals which irritate the mouth and throat.	Wash. Remove stems, put leaves together and roll up. Store in plastic bag in refrigerator or wrapped in a banana leaf in a cool place.	Cook leaves in boiling salted water for 5 minutes, turn over and cook for another 5 minutes. Drain and add butter or coconut cream. Reheat before serving. Cook leaves in boiling coconut cream as above. Serve in cream. Prepare Palusami (p. 101) or Palusami Casserole (p. 100). Prepare Chicken Rou Rou Casserole (p. 113) or Rou Rou Veal (p. 97). Prepare Fish in Rou Rou Leaves (p. 83) by wrapping around fish. Serve cold in Rou Rou Salad (pp. 53, 59).

Variety	Selection	Storage	Preparation and Uses
STARCHY ROOTS AND FRUITS			
BREADFRUIT	Fruit should be fully formed and firm. A pale yellow green in colour.	Keep cool to prevent further ripening. Store in a bucket of water or refrigerator. Half ripe fruit keeps for 1 or 2 days. Ripe fruit is soft and has a sweet flavour.	Peel, cut in wedges, remove seeds and steam or boil. Wash, puncture with a skewer and bake in 350° F oven for 1 to 1½ hours or until soft. Test with a skewer. Cut in wedges and serve with butter. An attractive dish for a buffet meal. Cook whole fruit over hot coals, turning frequently. Breadfruit cooked by this method has a very good flavour. Prepare Stuffed Breadfruit (p. 169) or make Breadfruit Pastry (p. 147). Prepare Breadfruit Chips (p. 24) with cooked breadfruit. Prepare breadfruit salad with Prawn Tafolu (p. 55).
COOKING BANANAS (Vudi, Plantains)	There are many varieties. Use green, half-ripe and ripe.	Hang a bunch in a cool place.	Steam, boil or bake in the skin. Peel before serving. Peel green and fry as Chips (p. 25). Half cook, peel and then roast in hot fat or oil and serve with meat. Use in place of bananas in Banana Meat casserole (p. 171). Serve ripe with coconut cream.
CASSAVA (Tapioca, Tavioka, Manioc)	Break a root to see that it is white inside and does not contain hard fibres. Blue streaks in the flesh indicate that roots are not fresh. Bitter cassava has a smell of almond essence. This is poisonous.	Freshly dug cassava will last for 2–3 days when stored in a cool place.	Peel, cut into 3 to 4 inch lengths and boil or steam. Make grated raw cassava into small crisp Cassava Drops (p. 25). Mash cooked cassava, combine with meat, fish or onion and seasonings as in Cassava Cakes (p. 170). Prepare desserts with grated raw cassava as in Lote Supreme and Variations (p. 126).

	Selection	Storage	Preparation
KUMALA (Kumara, Sweet Potato)	A number of varieties are available. Choose roots that are sound and free from holes. The kumala is frequently attacked by a borer insect. White-fleshed kumala is less sweet than the yellow varieties. The latter have a higher food value.	Store on open wire shelves. Kumala keeps for 3-4 weeks or more.	Scrub well and steam or boil in the skin. Peel when cooked and serve with melted butter and chopped parsley. Use cold kumala in Spiced Kumala and Banana Salad (p. 55). Peel, parboil and place in hot fat or oil and roast. Excellent served with pork. Cook and mash with butter, salt and pepper or prepare Scalloped Kumala (p. 170). Prepare Glazed Kumala (p. 170) and serve with pork. Prepare Kumala Pie (p. 131) or Kumala Soufflé (p. 170). Bake kumala in its skin, scoop out flesh and mash with a little butter and port wine. Season with salt and pepper. Refill shells and brown in hot oven.
KAWAI (Sweet yam)	Choose firm clean roots.	As for kumala. Kawai will keep for several months.	Scrub, cut off the hairs, punch holes in skin with skewer and bake. Serve with butter. Peel and steam or boil.
TARO (Dalo)	There are numerous varieties, some have a white dry texture when cooked, others have flesh of a blue grey colour and cheeselike texture. Seek local advice on a variety to your liking. Roots should be freshly dug and must be firm to the touch.	Keep in a cool dry place. Roots stay in good condition for 3-4 days.	Peel and bake whole in the earth oven "lovu" or cut in halves and bake in the oven. Serve with butter. Cut in slices and steam or boil. Prepare cooked taro into Chips (p. 24).

Variety	Selection	Storage	Preparation and Uses
TARO (Dalo ni tana)	The small potato sized roots should be firm and free from blemishes.	Store on wire racks. Roots keep for 2–3 weeks.	Peel and steam or boil.
YAMS	There are many kinds of yam grown in the tropics. Yam flesh is either white or purple.	Store on wire shelves in a dark place. Yams keep for several months.	Scrub and bake whole. Cut off the top, scoop out the flesh and mash with milk, butter and seasonings. Refill and brown in oven. Peel, steam or boil and cut in slices. Top with butter and garnish with parsley.

Hot beans

prepared mustard
sugar
butter
salt
lemon juice
vinegar
cooked green beans
Serves: 6

Mix 1 T prepared mustard, 1 T sugar, 2 T butter and ½ t salt in a saucepan. Heat slowly, stirring well. Add 1 T lemon juice and 1 T vinegar. Stir well. Pour over 3 c cooked green beans. Blend well.

Eggplant and olives
(Chinese marrow is equally good instead of eggplant)

eggplant or Chinese
  marrow
water
salt
onion
garlic
green pepper
celery (optional)
butter
chilli sauce
cheese
olives
salt and pepper
chopped parsley
Serves: 6

Peel 1 lb (½ kg) eggplant or about 1½ lb (¾ kg) Chinese marrow. Cut in ½ inch cubes. Cook till just tender in boiling salted water. Finely chop 1 medium onion and crush 1 or 2 cloves of garlic. Chop 1 green pepper and 1 or 2 celery stalks if liked. Sauté chopped vegetables and garlic in 2 T butter for about 5 minutes. Stir in 1 or 2 t chilli sauce. Combine with eggplant or Chinese marrow. Lastly fold in 1 c grated cheese and ½ c chopped ripe olives and season to taste with salt and pepper. Place in baking dish and cook at 300° F till thoroughly heated. *Variation:* Omit cheese and add ¾ c chopped tomato to sautéd vegetables.

Scalloped eggplant or Chinese marrow

eggplant or Chinese
  marrow
salted water
white sauce
cheese
onion
breadcrumbs
Serves: 6

Peel 1 lb (½ kg) eggplant or 1½ lb (¾ kg) Chinese marrow. Slice and cook in boiling salted water until just soft. Drain.
Add ¼ c grated cheese to 1 c White Sauce (p. 26) plus 1 small finely grated onion. Place eggplant in baking dish, pour over sauce, sprinkle with ¼ c dried breadcrumbs mixed with ¼ c grated cheese.
Bake at 350° F until brown.
Vary this dish by adding alternate layers of eggplant, sliced tomato and chopped green pepper or use cooked fish in alternate layers.

167

Stuffed eggplant

eggplant
onion
garlic
oil
minced beef
parsley
salt
pepper
rice or crumbs
tomato purée
egg
Serves: 3 to 6
  depending
  size of eggplant

Cut 3 medium eggplant in half and scoop out the flesh, leaving $\frac{1}{4}$ inch around the sides.
Finely chop 1 medium onion and crush 1 garlic clove. Measure $\frac{1}{4}$ c oil. Sauté onion and garlic in $\frac{1}{2}$ of oil in saucepan. Add $\frac{1}{2}$ lb ($\frac{1}{4}$ kg) mince and chopped flesh of eggplant. Sauté for 3 to 5 minutes. Season with 1 T chopped parsley, 1 t salt and $\frac{1}{2}$ t white pepper. Stir in $\frac{1}{4}$ c cooked rice or dried breadcrumbs and 2 T tomato purée. Cook for 2 to 3 minutes. Remove from heat and beat in 1 egg.
Arrange eggplant shells in a casserole. Fill with mixture. Pour remaining oil over. Cover with lid or aluminium foil and bake in moderate oven, 350° F for 1 hour.
Equally good hot or cold.
Note: Left overs like baked beans, tinned spaghetti, meat sauce may be used in this recipe.

Okra gumbo

bacon
onion
green pepper
okra
tomato
tinned sweet corn
salt and pepper
Serves: 6

Chop 1 rasher of bacon. Fry over medium heat until slightly crisp. Slice onions to yield $1\frac{1}{2}$ c and finely chop green pepper to yield $\frac{1}{2}$ c. Add to bacon and sauté for 5 minutes.
Slice 18 young well scrubbed okra pods. Peel and quarter 5 large tomatoes (yield 2 c). Add to onion and green pepper. Simmer for 10 minutes or until dry. Stir in 1 c well drained tinned sweet corn. Season to taste with salt and pepper. Cover and simmer for 15 minutes.
Excellent served with lamb, beef or corned beef.

Savoury spinach dish

spinach
butter
onion
garlic
salt
pepper
eggs
soft breadcrumbs
cheese
Serves: 6

Any soft green leafy vegetable may be used, e.g. spinach or other green leaves like rou rou.
Prepare 1½ lb (¾ kg) green leaves. Melt ¼ c butter in saucepan. Add ½ c chopped onion, 1 clove crushed garlic, spinach, ½ t salt and ¼ t pepper. Cook with lid on until spinach is soft. Remove the lid and cook until moisture has evaporated. Cool. Combine spinach with 2 well beaten eggs. Place in baking dish. Brown ½ c soft breadcrumbs in a little butter. Combine with ¼ c grated cheese and sprinkle over spinach.
Bake in moderate oven (350° F), for 45 minutes.

Stuffed breadfruit

breadfruit
spring onions
onion
green pepper
oil
parsley
mixed herbs
leftover meat
beef stock
salt
pepper
Serves: 6 to 8

Wash and dry 1 large breadfruit. Pierce well with a fork. Bake in 350° F oven for 1½ hours or until just soft.
Sauté 2 chopped spring onions, 1 medium sized chopped onion and 1 chopped green pepper in 2 T oil for 3 to 4 minutes. Add 2 T chopped parsley and 1 T chopped fresh herbs, or ½ t dry herbs. Cook 1 minute more. Add 1 c cooked chopped meat (chicken, ham, beef, bacon or corned beef), 1 c beef stock and salt and pepper to taste. Cook for 15 minutes or until just moist. Cut a small slice off top of breadfruit. Scoop out pulp, leaving a ½ inch thick shell. Combine pulp and meat mixture, Refill breadfruit, replace top and wrap in aluminium foil. Bake in hot oven (400° F) for 30 to 40 minutes.
Cut in crosswise slices and serve with mushroom or brown sauce flavoured with chopped green pepper.

169

Cassava cakes (tapioca)

cassava
onion
parsley
cooked minced
  meat or
  cooked fish
egg
flour
Serves: 6

Mash 2 c cooked cassava. Add 2 t grated onion, 2 t chopped parsley, 1 c cooked minced meat or flaked fish and 1 well-beaten egg. Mix well. Season with salt and pepper.
Form into cakes and roll in flour. Fry in hot oil or fat till golden brown.
Variation: Omit fish or meat and add extra cup mashed cassava. Serve cakes as a vegetable.

Kumala (sweet potato) soufflé

butter
milk
onion
cinnamon
salt and pepper
cooked kumala
eggs
Serves: 6

Add 2 T melted butter, 1 T milk, 2 t grated onion, $\frac{1}{2}$ t powdered cinnamon and salt and pepper to taste, to 3 c cooked mashed kumala.
Separate 2 eggs. Beat yolks and stir into kumala. Beat whites until stiff and fold into mixture. Place in buttered baking dish. Brush the top with oil or melted butter. Bake at 325° F in pan of water for 45 minutes or until puffy and golden. Serve with pork dishes or cold meats.

Scalloped kumala (sweet potato)

kumala
seasoned flour
milk
nutmeg
butter
Serves: as desired

Peel kumala. Cut in $\frac{1}{8}$ inch slices. Shake kumala in bag with seasoned flour. Arrange slices in a baking dish. Pour sufficient milk over kumala to just cover, dot with butter and sprinkle with grated nutmeg.
Bake at 300° F till kumala is soft (about 1 hour).

Glazed kumala (sweet potato)

brown sugar
butter
water
salt
kumala
Serves: 6

Bring 1 c brown sugar, $\frac{1}{4}$ c butter, $\frac{1}{4}$ c water, $\frac{1}{2}$ t salt to a boil in a heavy frying pan. Add 6 medium sized peeled, parboiled kumalas. Cook slowly, turning occasionally, until kumalas are caramelized.
Serve with pork or ham.

170

Banana meat casserole

green bananas
(vudi)
water
onion
tomato
green pepper
oil
minced mutton
or beef
salt
pepper
peanut butter
Serves: 6

Peel and slice sufficient green bananas (long eating) or vudi, to yield 3 c (about 6). Cover with cold water and leave from 1 to 2 hours. Chop 1 medium onion, 2 medium tomatoes and 1 large green pepper. Sauté in 2 T oil in fry pan with ¼ lb (100 g) minced mutton or beef for 5 to 7 minutes. Add strained bananas and sauté for a further 3 to 4 minutes.

Add ½ c water and simmer for 15 minutes or until just about dry. Season to taste with salt and pepper and 2 t peanut butter.

Place in a baking dish and cook in 350° F oven for 10 minutes.

An excellent luncheon dish.

Accompaniments

172

Many simple dishes are enhanced by the addition of an attractive accompaniment.
Fruit jellies and chutneys go well with hot and cold meats. A curry served with a variety of fresh vegetable chutneys, becomes a highlight of the menu. In this chapter, we are introducing some reliable but simple recipes for jams, jellies, sauces and chutneys. These will help to "dress up" the basic dish.
Many tropical fruits make excellent jams, jellies, pickles and chutneys.
Jams and jellies are more difficult to store in hot climates. In order to keep jars for more than a month or two, these rules must be followed:

1. Clean glass jars must be sterilized by heating in an oven at 250° F.
2. The boiling jams or jellies should be poured into hot jars and covered with a clean cloth. When partly cooled, sealed with boiling wax and then covered with greaseproof paper or damp Cellophane and a rubber band.
3. Jars should be stored in a cool airy cupboard.
4. Dust the jars regularly to prevent mould forming on the lids or paper covers.

Jellies

Excellent jelly can be made from these fruits: guava, mango, wi (spondius dulsis), Indian cherry (eugenia uniflora) Java or Brazilian cherry (slacortia inermis), yellow mangostene, lemons, limes, cumquats, and passionfruit, rosella (hibiscus sabdariffa).

Basic jelly

Wash and remove stalks and blemishes from half ripe fruit. Slice large fruits. Include the seeds with the flesh. Put fruit in a large pot and add sufficient water to

173

half cover the fruit. Bring to the boil and cook till fruit is soft and mushy. Strain through jelly bag made of linen, nylon or double butter muslin.

For high acid fruits—Indian and Brazilian cherry, wi, and mango, mangostene and citrus—add 1 c sugar to every cup of juice. For low acid fruits—guava, passionfruit and rosella—use $\frac{3}{4}$ c fruit juice and $\frac{1}{4}$ c lemon juice to 1 c sugar. Stir well till sugar is dissolved and mixture boils. The mixture should not be allowed to boil before the sugar has dissolved.

Put 6 c juice in a pan with 6 c sugar. Boil rapidly till a skin forms on a teaspoonful of jelly placed in a saucer (222° F). Remove white scum as this forms during cooking. It is important to cook jelly in small quantities; six cups is the maximum amount for a successful boiling.

Indian cherry

Contains plenty of pectin and sets easily. Goes well with lamb.

Java or Brazilian cherry

Makes one of the best tropical jellies. It has a dark red colour and has a fine tart flavour. Excellent as a spread or with meats.

Rosella

Has a red colour and mild flavour. Serve with meats or as a spread.

Wi

This fruit produces a pale pink juice very similar to apple juice. It contains plenty of pectin and sets easily. Very similar in flavour to apple jelly. Wi fruit can be added to guava to assist setting.

Guava

Produces a light red juice with a fine distinctive flavour. Guavas do not contain sufficient acid to obtain a set. Lemon juice or other acid fruit must be included in the recipe. If the ripening season has been very wet, reduce the amount of water when boiling fruit.

Passionfruit

Remove pulp from fruit, cut up skins, just cover with water and boil for about half an hour. Strain off water and add to pulp juice. Boil for a few minutes and then strain. For a tart flavour add 1 T lemon juice to 1 c passionfruit.

Mango

Use green or half ripe fruits, peel and cut in slices, remove the stones from green mangoes as they have a bitter flavour. Mango juice contains plenty of pectin. The jelly has a clear light yellow colour with an acid flavour. Suitable for spreads or meats. May be flavoured with mint or lemon.

Jams

Fruit salad jam

wi or green mangoes
bananas
pineapple
pawpaw
passionfruit
orange rind
lemon
sugar

Prepare and boil 8 medium sized wi fruit or green mangoes, as for jelly. Strain off the juice. Add 2 c sliced banana, 2 c finely cubed pineapple, 1 c cubed ripe pawpaw, $\frac{1}{2}$ c passionfruit pulp, grated rind of 1 orange and 2 T lemon juice, to the juice. Bring fruit to the boil and cook for 5 minutes. Remove and measure. Add 1 c sugar to every 1 c fruit pulp. Boil till sets. *Variation:* Use half rosella juice in place of part of guava or wi juice.

175

Guava jam

guavas
lemon juice
sugar

Prepare guavas as for jelly. Cook till soft, cool and rub fruit through a sieve or strainer. Measure the sieved pulp. Add $\frac{1}{4}$ c lemon juice to every 1 c pulp, then add 1 c sugar to every 1 c pulp and lemon juice. Stir frequently to prevent fruit from sticking to the pan. Boil until set.

Mango jam

mangoes
water
lemon juice
sugar
almonds
almond essence
(optional)

Peel 12 half ripe mangoes. Slice fruit and measure. Add $\frac{3}{4}$ c water and $\frac{1}{4}$ c lemon juice to every cup fruit. Place in saucepan, bring to a boil and simmer until fruit is soft. Cool and measure. Add 1 c sugar to every cup of fruit pulp. Add $\frac{1}{2}$ c peeled and chopped almonds, and, if desired, 2 t almond essence. Boil until jam sets.

Soursop jam

ripe soursop
sugar

Peel and sieve ripe soursop. Measure the pulp. Add 1 c sugar to every cup of pulp. Boil until mixture sets.

Citrus marmalade

Basic recipe.

grapefruit
oranges or
   cumquats
limes
water
sugar

Cut 2 small or 1 large grapefruit into quarters. Remove seeds and cut into thin slices. In a similar manner, slice 2 oranges or 8 cumquats. Peel the skin and pith off 4 limes. Cut flesh in thin slices. Place fruit in a bowl. Just cover with water and leave overnight. Boil until fruit skins are soft. Measure fruit. Add 2 c water and 3 c sugar to each cup of fruit. Place in large saucepan and boil until marmalade sets.

Note: For a tart flavoured marmalade, replace 1 c water with 1 c lemon or lime juice. The flavour of this recipe may be varied by using other combinations of citrus fruits.

Chutneys
COOKED
Basic mango chutney

mangoes
salt
water
pickling spice
chillies
green ginger
malt vinegar
sugar
Yield: 8 cups

Mangoes should be firm with pale yellow flesh. Peel and slice sufficient to yield 5 lb (about 12 loosely packed cups). Soak in brine of $\frac{1}{3}$ c salt to 8 c water overnight. Drain well.

Prepare a cloth spice bag containing 3 level T pickling spice, 4 to 5 small chopped chillies (6 if you like it hot) and 2 T peeled green ginger which has been mashed with salt until a pulp has formed. Tie securely with a string.

Bring 1 pint (510 ml) malt vinegar to a rapid boil, add spice bag and cook for 3 to 4 minutes. Add $6\frac{1}{2}$ c sugar, stir till dissolved, then boil. Add mango pulp and return and bring to boil as fast as possible. Cook for 2 minutes, then remove any scum that has formed on top. Cover and reduce heat to simmer. Stir occasionally and cook until mangoes are easily pierced with a fork.

When done the syrup will be clear and mangoes will be soft and partially transparent. Do not wait until all the mango is transparent before removing as this could result in over-cooking and a cloudy syrup. Remove from heat, remove spice bag, cool slightly and pack into sterilized jars.

This moderately hot chutney, with a smooth mellow flavour, goes well with curry, or as a relish with cold meat.

Hot sweet chutney

pineapple, mango or wi
sugar
vinegar
green ginger

Peel pineapple, mango or wi. Cut into cubes or slices. Weigh. Add 1 lb ($\frac{1}{2}$ kg) sugar, 3 c vinegar, 2 T finely chopped green ginger, 3 crushed garlic cloves, 2 large finely chopped onions, 2 T salt,

M

177

garlic
onions
salt
lemon rind
cinnamon stick
chillies (optional)

grated rind of 1 lemon, 1 2-inch stick cinnamon and 2 to 3 small seeded chopped chillies (optional) to every 2 lb (1 kg) prepared fruit.
Place all ingredients in a large saucepan and simmer until mixture thickens.
Serve with lamb or pork.
Variation: Add ½ c chopped almonds and 1 c raisins or sultanas towards the end of cooking time.

Hot spicy tomato chutney

cumin seed
fenugreek seed
mustard seed
salad oil
garlic
green ginger
tomato
turmeric
salt
tamarind
water
coriander leaves
Yield: 2½ cups

Sauté ¼ t cumin, ½ t fenugreek and ½ t mustard seed in 2 T hot salad oil in a saucepan, for 2 to 3 minutes.
Crush 1 clove garlic and 1 1-inch piece of peeled green ginger. Add to spices and sauté for a further 2 to 3 minutes. Add 2½ c chopped tomato or one large tin tomatoes, 14–16 oz. Season with ½ t turmeric and salt to taste. Blend well.
Mix 1 t tamarind pulp with 1 T water. Chop 2 T coriander leaves. Add tamarind and coriander to chutney. Cook for 10 to 12 minutes. Pour into hot sterilized jars and seal. Serve with curries, cold meat or pilau.
Variation: Add 1 medium chopped onion. Replace tamarind pulp with 1 T lemon juice.

FRESH CHUTNEYS
Cucumber chutney

cucumber
chillies
onion
salt
vinegar or
   lemon juice
Yield: 1 cup

Peel and coarsely shred 1 small cucumber and drain off juice. Remove the seeds and finely chop 1 to 2 chillies. Finely chop enough onion to yield 1 T. Add chilli, onion, ½ t salt and 2 t vinegar or lemon juice to cucumber. Chill for 2 to 3 hours. Serve with curries and fish dishes.

178

Coconut chutney

coconut
chillies
parsley or
  coriander leaves
salt
Yield: 1 cup

Finely chop 1 c freshly grated coconut. Remove the seeds and finely chop 1 to 2 chillies. Chop 1 T parsley or coriander leaves. Place all ingredients in a bowl with 1 t salt and 1 T lemon or tamarind juice. Blend well and leave for 1 to 2 hours to allow flavour to develop before serving.
Serve with curries.
Variation: Substitute similar quantity finely chopped mint for parsley or coriander leaves or 1 finely chopped medium tomato for lemon juice.

Tomato chutney

tomato
onion
chillies
garlic
coriander leaves
salt
Yield: 2 cups

Finely chop sufficient tomatoes to yield $1\frac{1}{2}$ c. Grate 1 small onion. Place 1 to 2 chillies, 1 clove garlic and $\frac{1}{2}$ c coriander leaves on a board. Sprinkle with salt. Crush with a wooden rolling pin. Blend well with tomato and onion.
Note: Coriander leaves, chilli, garlic and salt may be crushed in a blender.
Serve with curries.

Sauces

Fruit sauce or ketchup

green mangoes,
  guavas, tomatoes
  or other fairly
  acid fruit
water
vinegar
sugar
salt
allspice, powdered
mixed spice
cinnamon
cloves

Place clean chopped green mangoes, guavas, tomatoes or other fairly acid fruit in a saucepan with sufficient water to just cover. Boil until soft and sieve, or purée in blender. To every 5 c fruit purée add 1 c vinegar, 1 c sugar, 1 T salt, 1 t ground allspice, 1 t mixed spice, 1 t cinnamon, 4 cloves, 1 c (150 g) finely chopped onion, 1 T pounded garlic, 1 T pounded green ginger, 2 to 3 finely chopped chillies, grated rind 1 small lemon or lime and 1 t monosodium glutamate.

179

onion	Combine all ingredients in a saucepan and
garlic	boil for 20 minutes. If mixture becomes too
green ginger	thick, add a little water. Pour into sterile
chillies	hot jars or bottles.
lemon or lime rind	*Note :* To speed preparation, place ginger,
monosodium	garlic and onion in blender with vinegar.
glutamate	This sauce stores well. Excellent served
	with meat.

Chilli wine or vinegar

birdseye or other	Clean and remove stalks from birdseye or
hot variety of	other hot varieties of chillies. Cover the
chilli	chillies with white vinegar, dry sherry, or
white vinegar,	gin. Leave for several months.
dry sherry or gin	Use a few drops to flavour soups, stews or
	tomato dishes.

Other spicy sauces to serve with meats and vegetables come from
West Africa and Indonesia. Peanuts, tomatoes and chillies form
the basis of a number of sauces which are used with meat and
vegetables.
We hope the following recipes will add interest to plain meat or
vegetable dishes.

Fresh chilli tomato sauce—hot and spicy!

chillies	Wash $\frac{1}{2}$ c chillies. Remove seeds and cut
salad oil	into pieces. Place in a jar and cover with
garlic	salad oil. Leave for several days.
parsley	Crush chillies to a paste. Add 1 crushed
peanut butter	garlic clove, 1 T chopped parsley, $\frac{1}{2}$ c
tomatoes	peanut butter, and 6 medium tomatoes,
salt	peeled and chopped. Season with salt and
pepper	pepper. Blend until smooth.
Yield: 2 cups	Serve with steak, kebabs and savoury rice
	dishes.
	Note : This sauce will keep in the refrigera-
	tor for 2–3 weeks.

Pickled walnut sauce

pickled walnuts
peanut butter
tomato paste
chilli sauce
beef stock
salt
Yield: 1 cup

Grind 3 pickled walnuts to a smooth paste. Combine with ½ c peanut butter, 1 T tomato paste and 1 t chilli sauce. Place in a saucepan. Add beef stock until a smooth creamy consistency is reached. Simmer for 5 to 10 minutes. Season to taste with salt. Serve with steak and kebabs.

Peanut sauce

onion
green ginger
garlic
peanut oil
peanut butter
coconut cream
soy sauce
sugar
chilli
lemon juice
salt
Yield: 2½ cups

Finely chop 1 onion, 1 t green ginger and crush 2 garlic cloves. Sauté in peanut oil until golden brown. Add 4 T peanut butter and 2 c coconut cream. Blend well. Season with 2 T soy sauce, 2 t sugar, 1 chopped seeded chilli, 1 T lemon juice and salt to taste. Stir well and simmer for 5 to 10 minutes.
Serve with kebabs and rice or with vegetables.
Variation: Add 1 T tomato paste.

Miti

coconut
lemon
chillies
onion
salt
Yield: ½ cup

Place 1 grated coconut in a bowl. Add 1 medium sliced lemon with skin on, 1 or 2 chopped chillies, 2 T finely chopped onion and 1 t salt. Blend well and leave for 1 to 2 hours. Squeeze out coconut cream using the hands. Strain.
Variation: Add 1 c water to coconut before squeezing. This makes a weaker sauce.

Pickles

Hot spicy lime pickle

limes
salt
turmeric
garam masala or
  curry powder
chilli powder
green chillies

Cut 2 lb (1 kg) limes into 8ths. Mix together 4 T salt, 1 t turmeric, 2 t garam masala or curry powder, 1 to 2 t chilli powder, depending on taste, and 2 to 3 chopped green chillies. Add limes and blend well. Place in clean screw top jar and cover. Keep in a warm place for a week, shaking the jar every day. The pickle is ready to use when the lime skin is soft. Serve with curries.
Variation: Add 6 oz (150 g) sugar to basic recipe.

Plain lime pickle

limes
salt
turmeric
lime juice

Cut limes into quarters almost to the base. Fill the centre with salt and turmeric in the ratio of 1 t turmeric to 1 oz (25 g) salt. Pack "stuffed" limes into clean jars. Add sufficient fresh lime juice to cover fruit. Cover jars and place in a warm place. Shake daily. It will be ready to use when the lime skins are soft.
Serve with fish curry and fish dishes.

Oriental vegetable pickle

carrots
white radishes
cucumbers
water
sugar
salt
vinegar

Peel and thinly slice 1 lb carrots and 1 lb white radishes. Cut 1 lb cucumbers into pieces 2 inches long and $\frac{1}{4}$ inch thick. Pack sliced vegetables into clean jars. Bring 2 c water, 3 c sugar, $\frac{1}{4}$ c salt and 2 c vinegar to a boil. Cool and fill jars, making sure that vegetables are completely covered. Cover and keep in cool place for at least 3 days before using. Store in refrigerator.
Serve as an accompaniment to sweet and sour dishes.

Fresh cucumber pickle

cucumbers
salt
French dressing
chives or fresh dill

Peel and thinly slice 2 medium sized cucumbers. Sprinkle with 2 to 3 t salt. Place in a colander and leave to drain for 1 to 2 hours. Squeeze out any surplus moisture. Marinate in French Dressing (p. 50), to which 2 t chopped chives or fresh dill has been added. Serve with fish or egg dishes.

Fresh green pawpaw pickle

green pawpaw
vinegar
salt
green ginger
black pepper

Peel and remove the seeds from 1 medium sized green pawpaw (about 1 lb). Shred on a coarse grater. Place in a bowl and add 2 T white vinegar, 2 t salt, 1 t finely chopped green ginger and some freshly ground black pepper. Cover and store in refrigerator until ready to serve.
Serve as a pickle with cold meats and other cold dishes.

Index of recipes

184

185

187

188

189

190